Legal Issues in Integrative Medicine

A Guide for Clinicians, Hospitals, and Patients

Legal Issues in Integrative Medicine

A Guide for Clinicians, Hospitals, and Patients

Michael H. Cohen, J.D.

NAF
PUBLICATIONS

Gig Harbor, Washington

National Acupuncture Foundation
6405 43rd Avenue Ct NW, Ste B
Gig Harbor, WA 98335
(253) 851-6538
www.nationalacupuncturefoundation.org

Printed in the USA

ISBN: 0-9762537-0-4

Library of Congress Control Number: 2004115445

Cover design by Tierney Tully

If you are unable to order this book from your local bookseller, you may
order directly from the publisher. Quantity discounts for schools and organizations are available.

Notice: The information in this book is true and complete to the best of our
knowledge. It is offered without guarantee on the part of the author or the
National Acupuncture Foundation. The author and National Acupuncture
Foundation disclaim all liability in connection with the use of this book.

For Jessica Rafaelle
Welcome to this world, you are loved.

And for Elaine - my sacred mirror.

And for Perry, Margo, Daniel, Jonathan, Nancy
Ilana, Louis (Aryeh), Tillie, Louis J,
Betty, Ronald, and Judy.

For those who have come,
And, for those who are yet to come;
May you each receive infinite blessing,
And drink deep from the well of joy.

Contents

Foreword by
Sherman L. Cohn, J.D.

About thirty years ago, in my capacity as a lawyer, I was retained by two persons—Robert Duggan and Diane Connelly—who wanted to open a clinic in Maryland for the practice of acupuncture and a school for the education and training of acupuncture practitioners. Maryland was selected because it may have been the only state at the time that had a law authorizing the practice of acupuncture by non-physicians. The law had been enacted, without fanfare, as a result of the articles on acupuncture written by James Reston of the *New York Times*. Reston had accompanied President Richard Nixon to China and, in China, required an appendectomy. While hospitalized he experienced and observed the benefits of acupuncture.

This fortuity assisted to bring acupuncture to the United States. But, the Maryland statute had not yet been utilized. So, the first problem was a political one: the Maryland commission on higher education would not authorize any post-secondary education in a health-related field without guidelines from the Maryland Medical Examiners, and the Medical Examiners said they could give no guidelines in acupuncture because they knew nothing of the subject. It took a law firm with local political expertise to break through that "Catch 22." The breakthrough occurred and the Traditional Acupuncture Institute (now known as the Tai Sophia Institute) opened in 1975, as one of the first schools of acupuncture in the United States.

This was my first introduction to a form of health care outside of the allopathic model. I experienced the benefits in my own health care and I observed the beneficial effects on others. And, through an invitation to serve on the new national commission for accreditation of acupuncture and Oriental medicine colleges, of which I then served as chair for its first eleven years, I came to know and watch the birth of this new profession throughout the United States. Through this experience with acupuncture, I was introduced to, and came to know, other forms of alternative health care: chiropractic, naturopathy, reiki, Therapeutic Touch, and a dozen others. In recent years, I have worked together with practitioners of these other modalities in cooperative national settings.

During these thirty-five years, the health modality alternatives to our conventional, allopathic medicine have grown. In this time, use of alternative therapies has grown from a practice to be hidden and shunned to be very much in the forefront of exploration and of actual therapy. Studies published in the *Journal of the American Medical Association* and in the *New England Journal of Medicine* show that Americans make more visits to alternative practitioners than to conventional, allopathic physicians, spending billions of dollars annually out of their own pockets for alternative health care. The National Institutes of Health now has a Center for Complementary and Alternative Medicine. The highly respected M.D. Anderson Cancer Center now has a highly regarded integrative cancer program. And, these are only a few of the many significant indications of change.

Indeed, hospitals are, to an increasing extent, adding alternative therapy practitioners: acupuncturists, massage therapists, Therapeutic Touch practitioners, to name a few. Herbal remedies are being studied and offered in scores of centers around the nation. A significant number of physicians are now also certified in various alternative modalities. The American Medical Association (AMA), having been chastised by the courts in an antitrust action, is no longer in active opposition. And, there are more and more health-care offices in which healers of various modalities—including conventional physicians—work together in integrative fashion. While Ann Fonfa, the head of the Annie Appleseed Project (which presents the research across modality lines online at http://www.annieappleseedproject.org) states in the Nov/Dec 2004 issue of *Alternative Medicine*: "There's a lot of talk lately about integrative medicine. Unfortunately, a lot of it's just that, talk", Mayra Rodriquez Govannelli, M.D., Director of the Puerto Rico Complementary Foundation for Cancer and the Puerto Rico Reiki Institute, notes in an upcoming article: "There are many medical doctors who are accepting this integration . . ." Most mainstream medical schools, in the past few years, have begun integrating alternative medicine into their regularly required studies. The highly respected University of Pennsylvania School of Medicine has entered into a partnership with the Tai Sophia Institute by which medical students at the University will be offered the possibility of a joint degree, an M.D. from the University of Pennsylvania and a Masters in Integrative Medicine and the Healing Arts from Tai Sophia.

There is truly movement and change. Unfortunately, change brings with it legal problems followed by regulatory issues. Alternative and integrated healing centers must be concerned about the law—law that is only now developing and is far from settled. There are legal problems that can, and do, arise. These problems arise whether the health care practitioner is a physician practicing an alternative modality, an alternative practitioner practicing independently, or whether the practitioner is working in an integrative setting.

The law, of course, keeps evolving. A few weeks before this Foreword was written, the Food and Drug Administration (FDA) announced a policy that, for the first time, appears to be implementing the power that it was given in the Dietary Supplement Health and Education Act (DSHEA) of 1994 to begin policing the dietary supplement industry. In addition, two additional jurisdictions (California and the District of Columbia) recently enacted legislation licensing naturopathic practitioners.

Michael H. Cohen, a lawyer who offered the first course in an American law school on the legal issues of complementary and alternative medicine, has now written four books on these issues. This, his latest book, is addressed to health care practitioners, to the administrators of alternative and integrative clinics and hospitals, and to patients. It is also very useful for the attorney who has had little or no experience in this field.

This book presents a road map of issues and approaches. It raises questions and points to the answers where answers exist. In that sense, it is a primer. In a new field, a primer is needed. This truly is a new field—not only of health care, but also of law and legal practice. As more and more alternative health care offices open, as there is more and more integration, clients—practitioners, administrators, and patients—approach their attorneys for guidance. But, as very few law schools even introduce the subject (as of this writing, this author knows of only three: Georgetown, Syracuse, and Seton Hall, with one now proposed at Houston), and established health law organizations (e.g., the American Bar Association's Health Law Section) have not yet begun to offer continuing education courses in this field, very few lawyers have the background to deal with these issues. This book will help those lawyers. And, it will help clients educate their lawyers on the issues they face.

As we see the world of health care evolving, we see alternative care increasingly in the picture. To a great extent, the movement is led by those consumers who are demanding more and are not willing to accept the paternalistic answers of old. But, it is the practitioner, the administrator, the clinic, the hospital, and their lawyers, who must struggle with the legal issues. This book is a place to start.

Sherman L. Cohn, J.D.
Chevy Chase, Maryland
November 2004

Acknowledgements

A work emerges from many minds and much support.

My gratitude flows to each and every influence. I thank Alan Dumoff, J.D., an attorney in Rockville, Maryland who specializes in CAM legal issues, and Cynthia Bowkley, J.D. for invaluable comments on the manuscript. I appreciate the fellowship of Sherman Cohn, J.D. and his willingness to provide an introduction. Tierney Tully conceived the book's cover design, for which I am grateful.

I thank the Greenwall Foundation and the Rudolph Steiner Foundation for support.

I thank my wife, Elaine F. Kerry, for constant encouragement. Family and friends too numerous to mention have helped in innumerable ways. My gratitude also goes to Castor and Pollux for the endless delight and the contribution of their dancing keyboard paw-prints to the manuscript. And finally, with great love, I welcome Ujayi.

Introduction

The purpose of this book is to empower you to make better decisions concerning the health care services that you, as a health care professional or health care institution, either recommend or provide to your patients, or that you, as a patient, choose for yourself or your family. Specifically, this book addresses legal issues involved in providing (or seeking) complementary and alternative medicine (CAM) therapies.

Although many definitions for CAM therapies exist, a helpful working definition is: "a group of diverse medical and health care systems, practices, and products that are not presently considered to be part of conventional medicine."[1] This includes therapies such as chiropractic naturopathy, massage therapy, acupuncture and traditional oriental medicine, nutritional and herbal medicine, folk medicine, mind–body therapies, and various forms of spirituality in medicine.

These therapies increasingly are becoming part of health care services offered in conventional medical settings, and are used independently by millions of people. Today, at least somewhere between one-third to one-half of Americans use CAM therapies; a recent survey found a 47% increase in total visits to complementary and alternative medicine practitioners, from 427 million in 1990 to 629 million in 1997, with total 1997 out-of-pocket expenditures relating to alternative therapies estimated at 27 billion dollars.[2] The study suggested that use of complementary and alternative medicine is likely to continue to increase, particularly as insurance reimbursement for complementary and alternative therapies grows.[3]

In similar fashion, a survey by the American Hospital Association reported that, of the respondents, 15% offered CAM therapies, such as pastoral care, massage therapy, relaxation treatment, guided imagery, therapeutic nutrition, naturopathy, homeopathy, chiropractic, and reflexology.[4] Medical schools have begun offering elective courses to train physicians regarding use of CAM thera-pies.[5] An office within the National Institutes of Health to research CAM therapies, created by Congress in 1992, has grown into the National Center for Complementary and Alternative Medicine (NCCAM), with an annual research budget of over $100 million.

The legal and regulatory landscape surrounding CAM thera-pies has grown more complicated in recent years, challenging cli-nicians and health care institutions, patients and their families, and those involved in the business of providing CAM products to consumers. For instance, legal rules governing dietary supple-ments often are difficult to decipher. On the federal level, the law regulating what kinds of claims manufacturers can make on dietary supplement labels has become increasingly complex. As an example, under current Food and Drug Administration (FDA) rules, one may claim a product is "for the relief of occasional sleeplessness," but not that it "helps you fall asleep if you have trouble falling asleep." The first is considered an acceptable "struc-ture-function claim," and the second, an unacceptable "disease claim."

Clinicians and institutions, called on to counsel patients about dietary supplements, must sort through this information, while patients must understand these different claims, and why the law allows them to access some CAM therapies (such as dietary supplements) but not others that lack FDA approval.

On the state level, in the past several years, many new laws have granted licensure to CAM practitioners such as naturopaths, acupuncturists, and massage therapists, and at least three states have enacted laws allowing CAM practitioners with-out licensure— such as non-physician homeopaths and practi-tioners of reiki who are not otherwise independently licensed—to deliver health care services. At the same time, a number of cases have addressed the malpractice liability practitioners might face when recommending CAM therapies to their patients.

On the front of professional and administrative regulation, there are new model guidelines by the Federation of State Medical Boards letting physicians know what they must do when counseling patients about use of CAM therapies. And apart from these rules, many physicians and institutions have begun to implement "integrative health care," which "combines mainstream medical therapies and CAM therapies for which there is some high quality scientific evidence of safety and effectiveness."[6] Many hospitals are beginning to open centers for integrative care, in which conventional and CAM practitioners are expected to operate as a team.

In short, we are in the midst of a dynamic, rapidly changing environment for CAM therapies. This book provides basic but essential guidance for those seeking to understand the legal context in which they offer health care services involving CAM therapies, refer patients to CAM practitioners, or use such therapies themselves.

This book also is addressed to patients who seek these services or advice about these services from their physicians, other practitioners, and health care institutions. Patients may wonder how far they can push the system in terms of their right to access CAM therapies. Particularly in the hospital setting, patients may be interested to learn what their physicians, and other conventional clinicians, might think about legal implications of their involvement with CAM therapies. Patients, as well, may wonder how far they can push hospital personnel to honor preferences and requests for CAM therapies such as dietary supplements.

Patients, as well as clinicians and institutions, also may wish to buy a copy of this book for their attorneys, and hopefully save hundreds, if not thousands of dollars, by educating their legal counsel about this specialty area of law.

The book is organized in three parts. Part One addresses issues of particular interest to clinicians, while Part Two, intended for hospitals, focuses on issues of credentialing practitioners, institutional malpractice liability, and crafting policies governing dietary supplements. Part Three addresses concerns of patients and their families.

References are provided throughout. These include a number of scholarly books and also articles (in the medical and legal literature), which can be explored by those who desire a more comprehensive perspective on the evolution of legal and medical authority as both endeavor to support a more holistic view of human health. In other words, in your hands is a book oriented toward practical questions, with reference to earlier academic works offering more in-depth scholarly treatment. The appendices in this book offer additional guidance and resources. This includes drafts of some potential forms that may offer some protection against liability risk, with the caveat that these are educational in nature and that readers are encouraged to consult attorneys for legal advice and opinion tailored to their individual circumstances, and which incorporate relevant legal rules in their state.

As suggested, this book is educational in nature and does not purport to give legal advice or opinion. Neither the text nor forms are intended as a substitute for legal advice. Although the book will offer a framework for analysis, clinical scenarios differ and results of claims are unpredictable. Both for preventative consultation, and in the case of litigation, the reader should consider consulting and retaining an attorney familiar with his or her specific situation and the laws in the relevant state or states. As well, the book neither advocates specific CAM therapies nor use of CAM therapies in general, but encourages the reader to consult medical advice for a given condition.

With these caveats in mind, ideally, this book will help practitioners and patients enter the arena of CAM therapies by pursuing care that will ultimately be viewed as clinically responsible, ethically appropriate, and legally defensible.

References for Introduction

1. National Center for Complementary and Alternative Medicine, "What Is Complementary and Alternative Medicine?" http://nccam.nih.gov/ health/-whatiscam/#sup2.

2. David M. Eisenberg, R. B. Davis, S. L. Ettner, S. Appel, S. Wilkey, Maria Van Rompay, and R. Kessler, "Trends in Alternative Medicine in the United States, 1990–1997: Results of a Follow-up National Survey," 280 JAMA 1569 (1998).

3. Id.

4. American Hospital Association (Health Forum), 2000-2001 "Complementary and Alternative Medicine Survey," Chicago: American Hospital Association (2002), http://www.hospitalconnect.com). See also John A. Astin, "Why Patients Use Alternative Medicine: Results of a National Study," 279 *Journal of the American Medical Association* 1548-53 (1998).

5. Miriam S. Wetzel, David M. Eisenberg, and Ted J. Kaptchuk, "Courses Involving Complementary and Alternative Medicine at U.S. Medical Schools," 280 JAMA 784 (1998).

6. NCCAM, *What Is Complementary and Alternative Medicine.*

Part One: Clinicians

Physicians and allied health professionals (such as nurses, psychologists, and physical therapists) who are asked to counsel their patients about use of CAM therapies, offer such therapies to their patients or refer their patients to CAM providers, often ask the following questions:

- *Will I likely get sued if I offer my patients CAM therapies?*

- *Is it legally safe to refer my patient to a CAM practitioner? Does that practitioner have to be licensed?*

- *How do I structure my practice so that I minimize the risk of malpractice liability?*

- *When do I risk losing my license? What practices are likely to get me in trouble with the state medical (or other regulatory) board?*

- *What are my ethical obligations? Is there an obligation of informed consent? What does it look like?*

- *What are my ethical obligations in general? What if the patient demands a therapy that lacks safety or efficacy?*

CAM practitioners (such as chiropractors, acupuncturists, and massage therapists) often ask:

- *Am I held to the malpractice standards applicable to medicine? When do I risk professional discipline?*

- *What is my informed consent obligation?*

- *To what extent do I share liability with a medical doctor or another provider, if we are practicing "integrative" care?*

Chapters 1 and 2 address these questions.

Chapter 1

Physicians and Allied Health Professionals

Liability and Disciplinary Issues

Providing Patients CAM Therapies

Will I likely get sued if I offer my patients CAM therapies?

A patient could sue under several possible theories of liability, the most common of which are: (1) negligence (malpractice); and (2) fraud. Let's take malpractice first.

Malpractice (negligent practice) in health care is essentially defined as practicing below the standard of care, and by such conduct, injuring the patient.[1] Standards of care develop over time, by the interaction of leaders in a profession, reports in journals, discussions at professional meetings, and peer networks. The most common way to prove the standard of care at trial is for the plaintiff (who is suing) to introduce expert testimony to state what the standard of care is, and that the defendant (health care practitioner) failed to meet this standard. Defendant then will introduce expert testimony to the contrary, and typically, the jury must decide. Generally, the standard of care is specific to a profession (for example: medicine; physical therapy).

The problem is that, since CAM therapies historically have been defined as outside conventional standards of care, at least in the practice of medicine,[2] the potential arises to label use of such therapies as malpractice per se—that is, irrespective of any wrongdoing.[3] There are few reported judicial opinions in which patients have sued physicians or allied health professionals for malpractice, based on offering or counseling the patient about CAM therapies. This makes it difficult to predict results of future cases.

To date, at least one court, in *Charell v. Gonzales*, has articulated the proposition that a physician's inclusion of CAM therapies conceivably could itself be negligent, given the current definition of CAM therapies.[4] The court's conclusion is rather unfortunate, and leaves clinicians who counsel patients concerning choices involving CAM therapies without much guidance as to potential liability triggers.

Balancing the troubling conclusion in *Charell* is the fact that the decision is from a lower, New York court, and thus is not binding on other states; further, the court's assertion is known as dicta—that is, an opinion other than the "holding" or rule of law in the case—and thus not necessarily binding even on other New York courts.

Further, the particular facts of *Charell* may have played a role in the court's antipathy to CAM therapies. Among other things, the plaintiff's expert witness testified that the physician's choice of hair analysis and nutrition to treat cancer, was "bogus" and "of no value."[5] Defense counsel apparently did not introduce evidence to counter this attack, thus leaving the testimony without rebuttal. *Charell*, therefore, may not be a good predictor for future litigation.

Research suggests that the best way to prevent a malpractice case is to communicate effectively with the patient about the various therapeutic options, and their risks and benefits. Many malpractice lawsuits arise from miscommunication, misunderstanding, and subsequent hostility on the part of patients and their families who attribute an undesirable outcome to lack of proper care on the part of the practitioner. Clear communication with the patient reduces liability potential.

In addition to clear communication, there are a number of liability risk management strategies (discussed later in this chapter) that potentially can help lower legal risk when integrating CAM therapies. Finally, a number of legal defenses to malpractice may help a practitioner who is actually facing a lawsuit. These include the "respectable minority" defense—the idea that a significant segment within the profession accepts the modality, and assumption of risk—the notion that the patient knowingly, voluntarily, and intelligently assumed a risk of injury from the chosen therapy.[6] Although these defenses exist, their contours and availability vary by state. Moreover, most courts will not allow these defenses if the practitioner truly has been clinically irresponsible.

To at least offer some potential advantage that may be gained from these defenses, Appendix A offers a model form for documenting informed consent (discussed later in this chapter) and assumption of risk. The form is given with two caveats: (1) it should be reviewed and modified, as appropriate, by an attorney for a given situation, with legal advice and opinion (including as to its enforceability) in the practitioner's state; and (2) some courts will refuse to enforce releases of liability that attempt to bar recovery for medical malpractice.[7]

Moving from negligence to fraud, this claim, like negligence, is also a term of art with a specific legal definition: fraud means that a health care provider deceives the patient and does so with the intent to so deceive.[8] Sometimes therapies will be described in some opinion pieces within the literature as "fraudulent," but this often is simply rhetoric, much as the label of "quackery" was used historically to discredit practitioners outside of medical orthodoxy.

To constitute legal fraud, the deception has to be intentional (or at the very least, more than merely negligent) and not simply negligent or the result of an honest mistake or a reasonable difference between physicians.[9] Fraud suggests a higher level of culpability than negligence, and thus opens the defendant up to the possibility of punitive damages, on top of compensatory damages.

Referring Patients to CAM Practitioners

Is it legally safe to refer my patient to a CAM practitioner? Does that practitioner have to be licensed?

A 1998 study, published in the *Journal of the American Medical*

Association (JAMA), analyzed legal risk and liability issues surrounding physician referrals to (or co-managing of patients with) CAM practitioners. The study found that in general there are far fewer lawsuits and claims against CAM practitioners than against medical doctors, suggesting that referrals to CAM practitioners are less risky than might be imagined. For example, in 1995, there were .2 claims per 100 policyholders against massage therapists, 2.6 against chiropractors, and 9.0 against medical doctors.[10]

The authors attributed the "relative infrequency and lower severity of claims" against CAM practitioners to the relative noninvasiveness of most CAM therapies, and the "immature state of . . . claims consciousness outside conventional clinical medicine."[11] (Another factor, which the authors neglected to discuss, may have been the fact that CAM practitioners might have tended to be insured at lower levels than physicians, and thus to provide less attractive financial targets for injured patients.) Although they suggested that there might be more lawsuits in the future, the authors concluded that physicians who refer patients to CAM practitioners "should not be overly concerned about the malpractice liability implications of their conduct."[12]

The study pointed out that, while mere referral, without more, does not make a referring provider liable for the referred-to provider's negligence, this rule has several notable exceptions: (a) the referral itself is negligent, because it delayed necessary conventional care; and (b) the referring provider supervised the care, "jointly treated" the patient, or referred the patient to an incompetent provider.[13]

The liability risk management suggestions below address the first exception: clearly, the clinician should be wary of abandoning conventional monitoring and treatment, and be sure the referral does not delay necessary conventional care. Similarly, the clinician should take basic steps to become familiar with the CAM practitioner to whom the patient will be referred, and ensure that this practitioner is trained and skilled, and not obviously "incompetent."

Again, negligence means lack of due care, so the clinician has the obligation to take reasonable steps to ensure he or she is referring to someone competent. While it is difficult to determine exactly what a court later might consider reasonable and thereby sufficient, a few phone calls to relevant professional organizations, together with some calls to the practitioner and follow-up to gather documents that can help determine the practitioner's licensure, education and training, and clinical style, should help guard against a charge of referral to a known incompetent.

The other exceptions are more complex. Some states mandate supervision in certain circumstances (for example, physician supervision of non–M.D. acupuncturist), thereby creating an agency relationship, which means the physician could be liable for the supervisee's negligence. Similarly, where physicians (and allied health professionals) are collaborating with CAM practitioners in an "integrative" health care clinic, sharing diagnostic and treatment plans, they might be viewed as engaged in "joint treatment," and thereby share liability.

Again, a good liability management strategy is to become sufficiently familiar with the CAM practitioners with whom one shares patients so that, if the relationship is more than an arms-length referral, the referring provider has reasonable comfort about how the CAM practitioner is treating the patient. As the authors of the *JAMA* article conclude, the "same common sense considerations applicable to other [conventional medical] referrals will be a reasonably reliable guide regarding acceptable practice."[14]

In this regard, it may be more legally prudent to refer to licensed practitioners, since licensure typically signifies some state imprimatur of professional standards for education and training.[15] On the other hand, the law is in flux. At least three states—California, Minnesota, and Rhode Island—have enacted legislation authorizing non-licensed CAM practitioners to deliver health care services, so long as such practitioners do not act fraudulently, disclose their training and the fact that they lack

13

licensure, and meet other statutory requirements.[16] Clinicians should consult legal counsel familiar with the laws in their state, and also exercise common sense in deciding whether to make such referrals.[17]

Managing Potential Liability Exposure

How do I structure my practice so that I minimize the risk of malpractice liability?

The definition of malpractice given earlier is: practicing below the standard of care, which injures the patient. As suggested, attorneys for the plaintiff have a variety of ways to convince the jury that these elements have been satisfied.

One way for the defendant to convince the jury that giving the patient a specific, CAM treatment does not constitute practice below the standard of care, is to ensure that there is reasonable support in the medical literature regarding the therapy's safety and efficacy. In such a case, the medical expert for the defense would have ample basis for testifying that the therapy was well within accepted clinical practice. Furthermore, the defendant's choice of such therapy likely would appear not to create an unreasonable danger to the patient. In short, understanding the availability of evidence regarding safety and efficacy provides a good map to potential liability.

In this regard, one can think of a grid of clinical risk, with the x-axis indicating safety, and the y-axis, efficacy. Four quadrants indicate whether the medical evidence variously supports safety and/or efficacy, or is inconclusive regarding either:[18]

A. Supports safety and efficacy.

B. Supports safety, but evidence regarding efficacy is inconclusive.

C. Supports efficacy, but evidence regarding safety is inconclusive.

D. Indicates either serious risk or inefficacy.

Supports safety and efficacy. A	Supports safety, but evidence regarding efficacy is inconclusive. B
Supports efficacy, but evidence regarding safety is inconclusive. C	Indicates either serious risk or inefficacy. D

In quadrant A, the therapy by definition is unlikely to cause injury, and probably falls within the standard of care; its use therefore probably does not generate malpractice liability. In quadrant D, the therapy by definition is likely to cause injury and/or to fall below the standard of care; its use therefore probably does generate liability.

Most CAM therapies are likely to fall within quadrants B and C, in which either safety or efficacy concerns make the practitioner conceivably liable. Safety probably trumps efficacy, however, in that if a therapy is relatively safe, but the evidence regarding its efficacy is inconclusive, in general it would be more difficult to show that the therapy's use caused the patient injury (assuming an ineffective CAM therapy was not substituted for a conventional therapy deemed safe and effective). On the other hand, if evidence regarding safety is inconclusive and a patient is injured, it might be easier to assign the cause of the injury to the CAM therapy.[19]

A helpful way to help manage liability exposure is determine the clinical risk level, using the above grid. If the therapy falls within regions A, B, C, or D, a clinician respectively should: (A) recommend and continue to monitor; (B) accept use, caution the patient, and monitor effectiveness; (C) accept use, caution the patient, and monitor safety; and (D) avoid and actively discourage patient use.[20] The clinician should realize, however, that as medical evidence changes, therapies can shift from one quadrant to another.

In addition, the clinician can help manage potential liability by: (1) including a backup file of the literature supporting the therapeutic choice, and keeping clear notes in the medical record; (2) engaging the patient in a clear discussion of risks and benefits regarding the therapy, and if feasible, obtaining the patient's written, express agreement to use the treatment; and (3) continuing to monitor conventionally, and intervene conventionally when medically necessary.[21]

As an example, if the clinician recommends an herb, the clinician should, at a minimum, be certain there is no documented serious risk or proven inefficacy; document the choice of herb and rationale for this choice; and document any discussion regarding therapeutic dose, and any discussion with the patient concerning potential herb-drug interactions and other adverse effects or other therapeutic risks.

If the clinician is referring to (or co-managing the patient with) a CAM practitioner, a number of similar strategies are suggested. First, it probably will be helpful to know whether the CAM practitioner is using therapies that fall within an acceptable spectrum of risk in the grid. To the extent therapies fall in quadrant D, this is a "red flag" suggesting that referral may be inappropriate; while greater judgment is called for therapies in quadrants B and C.

Put another way, one should ask: "is there evidence from the medical literature to suggest that the therapies a patient will receive as a result of the referral will offer no benefit or will subject the patient to unreasonable risks?"[22] If the answer is yes, the referral may be inadvisable, as it could potentially subject the referring provider to an undesirable level of liability risk.

In addition, at a minimum, the clinician should review (or ask legal counsel to review) the licensing statute for that CAM practitioner and get a good feel for what services the practitioner can and cannot provide, and then inquire of any relevant licensing or regulatory body regarding the practitioner's history of malpractice litigation or disciplinary action.[23] It is also helpful to review one's own malpractice insurance policy and make appropriate inquiries to the carrier—and get answers in writing, if possible—

as to whether use of CAM therapies, referrals, and the like, will be covered, or are subject to specific exclusions.

Managing Risk of Professional Discipline

W*hen do I risk losing my license? What practices are likely to get me in trouble with the state medical (or other regulatory) board?*

Licensing statutes for health care professionals typically include a set of provisions specifying under what circumstances the licensed professional may be disciplined. These generally include: obtaining the license fraudulently, practicing the profession fraudulently, practicing with gross incompetence or gross negligence, practicing while impaired by drugs or alcohol, permitting or aiding an unlicensed person to practice unlawfully, or failing to comply with relevant rules and regulations. Sanctions for such "professional misconduct" (or "unprofessional conduct") range from fines to loss of licensure.

One of the provisions that have troubled providers who have offered CAM therapies is the medical boards' ability to strip a license for "any departure from acceptable and prevailing medical practice." This language was contained in a North Carolina licensing law, and challenged in the case of *In re Guess.*[24]

Guess was a family physician who used homeopathic remedies as a last resort, for patients when conventional therapies failed; he lost his license even though there was no evidence his treatments ever harmed a patient. Guess appealed the medical board's decision to the state superior court, which reversed the medical board, finding that decision to be "arbitrary and capricious." But North Carolina's Supreme Court reversed the superior court and reinstated the medical board's decision, on the basis that the language of the statute quoted above was broad enough for the board to strip Guess of his medical license, even without any showing of patient harm.[25]

The specific language of disciplinary provisions in licensing statutes varies from state to state, as do the ways courts are likely to interpret these statutes. North Carolina responded to the *Guess* decision by enacting legislation, providing that the medical board cannot revoke a person's license simply because the therapy departs from prevailing and acceptable practices, unless the Board establishes that the treatment "has a safety risk greater than the prevailing treatment or that the treatment is generally not effective."[26]

Similar laws (known to some as "health freedom" statutes) now exist in many states, including: Alaska; Colorado; Georgia; Massachusetts; New York; North Carolina; Ohio; Oklahoma; Oregon; Texas; and Washington.[27]

The language contained in these statutes varies by state. As an example, Colorado's statute provides: "The board shall not take disciplinary action against a physician solely on the grounds that such a physician practices alternative medicine."[28] This is a key provision, as it aims to prevent the arbitrary stripping away of licensure based on bias against use of CAM therapies.

Some states (or state medical boards), on the other hand, have language (in statutes or regulations, respectively) that may make it difficult for licensees to offer therapies such as homeopathy; for example, Kentucky and Illinois, proscribe use of "invalidated" therapies, and include in this prohibition the notion that use of an "implausible" therapy may trigger professional discipline.[29]

The Federation of State Medical Boards recently promulgated model guidelines to govern physician use of CAM therapies in medical practice.[30] The rules are quite detailed as to the criteria a medical board should use to determine whether a licensee using CAM therapies has committed professional misconduct. These rules emphasize, among other things: the need to use the "same standards of safety and reliability" for CAM as conventional diagnostic methods; documentation as to what medical options have been "discussed, offered, or tried, and if so, to what effect," and a statement as to whether certain options have been refused by the patient or guardian; a discussion of risks and benefits of therapeutic options; a determination as to whether the CAM therapy could interfere with conventional treatment; and a determination that the CAM therapy have a favorable risk-benefit ratio compared to other treatments for the same condition, be reasonably expected to result in a favorable patient outcome, and be likely to achieve greater benefit than no CAM treatment.

The Federation rules also provide that physicians may refer to CAM practitioners with the requisite skill and training, although the physician is responsible for monitoring results and should do so periodically to ensure progress is being achieved. The rules are specific about the required documentation in any case, and require that physicians understand the "medical scientific knowledge" associated with a CAM therapy. These rules have not been adopted in all states but rather are model guidelines for individual state medical boards to adopt, modify, or consider.[31] Again, regulations vary in each state, and it is important to engage legal counsel familiar with local law.

One of the other issues arising out of the Federation guidelines is that they do not necessarily track legal rules governing malpractice liability. While some of the liability risk management strategies given earlier in this chapter overlap with some of the Federation rules, in some cases the Federation rules are more demanding than liability rules or simply offer a different version of the safety/efficacy assessment suggested earlier.

In fact, malpractice liability and professional discipline involve two separate areas of law—the first, a lawsuit brought by an aggrieved plaintiff, and the second, a proceeding brought by a state regulatory board. Yet, while different, often these two proceedings can arise out of a single incidence of alleged negligence. Providers are cautioned to pay attention to both potential sources of legal trouble and adjust themselves accordingly.[32]

The Federation guidelines are relatively new and the extent of their influence remains to be seen. In the meanwhile, there are few, if any, recorded judicial opinions governing discipline of allied health professionals, such as psychologists, nurses, and physical therapists, for using CAM therapies. This is an area that may grow as CAM therapies increasingly penetrate care previously classified as "conventional." Despite the absence of much case law, however, some professionals have found themselves in difficulty for using some therapies—for example, nurses offering Therapeutic Touch in hospitals in which administrators have been adverse to this therapy.

In addition, there have been massage therapists, physical therapists, and other practitioners (both conventional and CAM) who have found themselves investigated by their regulatory boards for using reiki and other therapies.[33] It is important to know whether one's individual regulatory board has guidelines in place within the relevant state. In addition to consulting legal counsel, professional organizations can be a useful source of information regarding the existence, enforcement, and current interpretation of such rules.

Ethical Issues

Informed Consent

What are my ethical obligations? Is there an obligation of informed consent? What does it look like?

The standard for informed consent disclosure in conventional care is that the patient must receive whatever information is "material" to the patient's decision to undergo or forgo a particular treatment. One could assume that the same standard would apply to CAM treatment: the clinician offering CAM therapies presumably is obligated to disclose to patients all the risks and benefits of such therapies that are material to treatment decisions.[34]

Under this rule, there are two standards for judging materiality in informed consent: about half the states measure materiality by what a reasonable provider would consider important to the decision to undergo or forgo a particular treatment, while about half measure this by what the patient finds important. Typically, in addition to a discussion of risks and benefits, information that is required to be disclosed includes such matters as the inability of the provider to predict results, the irreversibility of the procedure (if this is applicable), the likely result of no treatment, and available alternatives.

Failure to provide adequate informed consent is a second theory supporting malpractice liability (in addition to negligent care). To date, no patient has successfully argued that a provider's failure to disclose the possibility of using a CAM therapy, instead of a biomedical therapy, caused injury and constituted malpractice. At least one court has, however, observed that such an argument would succeed if the therapy in question had a sufficient level of professional acceptance.[35]

This appellate decision suggests that CAM therapies that are well-supported by evidence of safety and efficacy are potentially material treatment options and that therefore, the availability of such therapies should be disclosed to patients, as well as pertinent potential benefits and risks. Clinical examples potentially include: use of acupuncture to reduce nausea following chemotherapy, which has been agreed to be effective by a National Institutes of Health Consensus Panel on Acupuncture; chiropractic care for acute low back pain; and mind-body techniques for chronic pain and insomnia.[36]

On the other hand, where patients are taking dietary supplements and receiving conventional, prescription medication, one could argue that informed consent implies a duty to inquire into the nature of those supplements, research any reported, adverse herb-drug interactions, and advise or warn the patient accordingly. For example, adverse effects have been reported involving the combination of St. John's Wort and the medication Indinavir in AIDS patients;[37] the duty of informed consent, therefore, likely includes a requirement that the clinician inquire into the patient's use of supplements and disclose such adverse effects where relevant.

Providing adequate informed consent, and documenting this process on a form developed from the one in Appendix A, does not necessarily mean that the interaction has satisfied legal requirements for assumption of risk, a defense to malpractice. Requirements for informed consent and for assumption of risk vary by state.

Many courts conflate and confuse the two doctrines—informed consent and assumption of risk—a confusion that is understandable if one considers that the two are related in terms of presuming clinician disclosure of risks and benefits. While the doctrines are distinct, Appendix A addresses the two by documenting that informed consent has taken place, and then adding optional, draft language for express assumption of risk.

Some courts will not allow patients to assume the risk of injury from choosing a CAM therapy. Moreover, simply signing a form does not necessarily mean that informed consent has taken place. Rather, the clinician must disclose the material risks and benefits of a treatment decision in a conversation with the patient, and thereby meet legal requirements of informed consent; the form merely offers a way to document that this process has occurred.

Ethical Concerns Generally

What are my ethical obligations in general? What if the patient demands a therapy that lacks safety or efficacy?

Informed consent is an ethical as well as legal obligation. Clinicians frequently ask to what extent patient requests regarding CAM therapies trigger ethical obligations—for example, how should a clinician respond if the patient insists on using a CAM therapy the clinician believes to be unsafe or ineffective?

One way to assess the ethical obligation is to consider and weigh the following factors: the severity and acuteness of illness; the curability of the illness by conventional forms of treatment; the degree of invasiveness, associated toxicities, and side effects of the conventional treatment; the availability and quality of evidence of utility and safety of the desired CAM treatment; the level of understanding of risks and benefits of the CAM treatment combined with the patient's knowing and voluntary acceptance of those risks; and the patient's persistent intention to use CAM therapies.[38] These factors present a sliding scale that allows a provider to variously recommend, accept the patient's use of, or proscribe CAM therapies.[39]

Thus, where the evidence is not compelling either for or against a particular CAM therapy, the clinician can follow the clinical risk spectrum presented earlier, and accept use, caution the patient, and monitor results.[40] But if the patient insists on using a CAM therapy the clinician believes to be unsafe or ineffective, then, as suggested earlier, the duty of informed consent requires disclosure of the therapy's material risks, including the evidence of lack of safety or of inefficacy. This, of course, puts an onus on the conventional provider to learn all he or she can about CAM therapies, so as to be able to advise the patient responsibly.

In any event, even if the physician disagrees with the patient's choice, the physician cannot simply abandon the patient. Rather, if the physician is the patient's primary care provider, the ethical duty of non-abandonment implies a "caring commitment" to the therapeutic relationship.[41] This means that the clinician should try to explain his or her viewpoint and help the patient in the decision making process, and only make an appropriate referral to another clinician after a dedicated effort to communicate, and if the physician's "own values compel such a decision."[42]

If the standard, conventional therapy is ineffective, then even a CAM therapy with little evidentiary support should be accepted, "because the patient has few, if any, good alternatives."[43] Ethically, the final choice of treatment "belongs to the patient," and should be honored, if at all possible, by the clinician.[44]

While the foregoing expresses a framework for ethical decision making based on medical evidence, sometimes, ethical norms operate on multiple levels, including manifesting respect for patient preferences and understanding that some CAM therapies (such as Tibetan medicine and traditional Oriental medicine) represent whole systems of medicine that "cannot—and should not—be presented out of context and captured within a mechanistic, reductionistic, and biopharmacological model of health."[45]

There is considerable debate in the literature regarding the extent to which conventional medical methodologies are appropriate to evaluate CAM therapies or require further adaptation, with strong arguments in both camps.[46] To some extent, this reflects a larger debate about the role of the humanities as opposed to the sciences in evaluating and legitimizing therapies. Ultimately, ethical dilemmas occur within the broader context of physical, mental, emotional, social, and spiritual dimensions of human health.[47]

References for Chapter I

1. Negligence, a tort, involves four elements: a duty owed by defendant to plaintiff, breach of that duty, injury to the plaintiff, and causation. Duty is easily shown since a health care provider typically has a legal obligation toward the patient to meet the standard of care. The formulation in the text combines the requirements of injury and causation.

2. Such a definition was proposed in a study of prevalence of alternative therapies in the U.S.: David M. Eisenberg, R. C. Kessler, C. Foster, F. E. Norlock, D. R. Calkin, and T. L. Delbanco, "Unconventional Medicine in the United States: Prevalence, Costs, and Patterns of Use," 328 *New Engl. J. Med.* 246, 256 (1993).

3. I offer more detail and analysis on this point in Michael H. Cohen, *Beyond Complementary Medicine: Legal and Ethical Perspectives on Health and Human Evolution*, 23-26 (Ann Arbor: University of Michigan Press, 2000). This and other referenced works by Michael.H. Cohen can be found through the Complementary and Alternative Medicine Law Blog, http://www.camlaw-blog.com."

4. *Charell v. Gonzales*, 660 N.Y.S.2d 665, 668 (S.Ct., N.Y. County, 1997). The decision was affirmed, but modified on appeal to vacate the punitive damages award, 673 N.Y.S.2d 685 (App Div., 1st Dept., 1998).

5. Id., at 669.

6. I discuss the potential application of these defenses in greater detail in Cohen (1998), at 58-59, 62-62, and Cohen (2000), at 26-31.

7. Maxwell J. Mehlman, "Informed Consent," http://www.thedoctorwillseeyou-now.com/articles/bioethics/consent).

8. Stuart M. Speiser et al., *The American Law of Torts*, § 32.1, at 207 (1992). I cite Speiser and discuss the applicability of tort rules for fraudulent conduct to use of CAM therapies in Michael H. Cohen, "A Fixed Star in Health Care Reform: The Emerging Paradigm of Holistic Healing," 27 *Ariz. L. J.* 79, 134-137 (1995).

9. The foregoing refers to civil fraud. Some regulatory boards still may be able to impose discipline based on charges of fraud, even if the elements of a civil case are not met. See the section infra on managing professional discipline.

10. David M. Studdert, David M. Eisenberg, Francis H. Miller, D. A. Curto, Ted J. Kaptchuk, and Troyen A. Brennan, "Medical Malpractice Implications of Alternative Medicine," 280 *JAMA* 1610, 1611 (1998).

11. Id.

12. Id., at 1614.

13. Id., at 1612.

14. Id., at 1614.

15. David M. Eisenberg, Michael H. Cohen, Andrea Hrbek, Jonathon Grayzel, Maria Van Rompay, and Richard M. Cooper, "Credentialing Complementary and Alternative Medical Providers," 137 *Ann. Int. Med.* 965 (2002).

16. CA *SB 577* (signed into law 9/23/02); *Minn. Stat.* § 146A; *R.I. Gen. Laws* § 23-74-1(3). I discuss some of these provisions in Michael H. Cohen, *Healing at the Borderland of Medicine and Religion: Regulating Potential Abuse of Authority By Spiritual Healers*, J. L. & Relig. (May 2003). I discuss some of the similarities and differences between "licensure" and "registration" in Cohen (1998), at 35–37. Many state agencies use the terms interchangeably.

17. See also the section infra on managing disciplinary proceedings, and in particular, the reference to the Federation of State Medical Board Guidelines (which, among other things, establish model rules for physician referrals to CAM practitioners).

18. The grid is adapted from a more comprehensive chart in Michael H. Cohen and David M. Eisenberg, "Potential Physician Malpractice Liability Associated With Complementary/Integrative Medical Therapies," 136 *Ann. Int. Med.* 596, 597 (2002). That chart was adapted for patients in a cover story entitled, "The Science of Alternative Medicine," in *Newsweek* (Dec. 2, 2002).

19. This analysis is presented in greater depth, with clinical examples, in Cohen & Eisenberg (2002).

20. Id., at 597–599.

21. Id., at 599–600.

22. This formulation is from Studdert et al. (1998), at 1614.

23. Cohen & Eisenberg (2002), at 601.

24. 393 S.E.2d 833 (N.C. 1990), cert. denied, *Guess v. North Carolina Board of Medical Examiners*, 498 U.S. 1047 (1991), later proceeding, *Guess v. Board of Medical Examiners*, 967 F.2d 998 (4th Cir. 1992).

25. I discuss this and related cases in more detail in Michael H. Cohen, "Holistic Health Care: Including Alternative and Complementary Medicine in Insurance and Regulatory Schemes," 38 *Ariz. L. Rev.* 1, (1996), 111–120, 149–153.

26. See id., at 152 (quoting N.C. Gen. Stat. § 90-14(a)(6)).

27. A list of current states is kept at http://www.healthlobby.com and at http://www.faim.org

28. *Colo. Gen. Stat.* § 12-36-117.

29. Kentucky Board of Medical Licensure, *Board Policy Statement: Complementary and Alternative Therapies (March 1999)*; Illinois Department of Professional Regulation Medical Disciplinary Board, *Board Policy Statement: Complementary and Alternative Therapies* (November 1999).

30. These rules are posted at http://www.fsmb.org, under Policy Documents.

31. In addition, the rules have been challenged on constitutional grounds. Comments are at http://www.apma.net/misc/FSMBletter.doc. For a commentary on the implications of these rules, see Alan Dumoff, "The Federation of State Medical Boards' New Guidelines for ACM Practice: Improvements and Concerns," 8(5) *Alt. & Comp. Therapies* 303 (2002).

32. Another excellent reference is Alan Dumoff, "Protecting ACM Physicians From Undeserved Discipline: Legislative Efforts in Maryland," 8(2) *Alt. & Comp. Therapies* 120 (2002).

33. See also the section in Chapter 2 on unlicensed medical practice, another issue that may affect non-physician providers who use CAM therapies at the borderland of medical practice.

34. Edzard E. Ernst and Michael H. Cohen, "Informed Consent in Complementary and Alternative Medicine," 161:19 *Arch. Int. Med.* 2288 (2001) (citing sources).

35. *Moore v. Baker*, 1991 U.S. Dist. LEXIS 14712, at *11 (S.D. Ga., Sept. 5, 1991), aff'd, 989 F.2d 1129 (11th Cir. 1993).

36. National Institutes of Health, "NIH Consensus Conference: Acupuncture," 280 (17) JAMA 1518 (1998); S. J. Bigos, O. R. Bowyer, R. G. Braen, K. Brown, R. Deyo and Scott Haldeman, *Acute Low Back Problems in Adults*. Clinical Practice Guideline (Number 14) (Rockville, Maryland: Agency for Health Care Policy and Research, US Dept. Health and Human Services, 1994); NIH Technology Assessment Statement, *Integration of Behavioral and Relaxation Approaches into the Treatment of Chronic Pain and Insomnia* (Bethesda, National Institutes of Health, 1995).

37. S. C. Piscitelli, A. H. Surstein, D. Chaitt, R. M. Alfaro, and J. Falloon, "Indinavir Concentrations and St. John's Wort," 355 *Lancet* 547(2000).

38. Karen E. Adams, Michael H. Cohen, Albert R. Jonsen, and David M. Eisenberg, "Ethical Considerations of Complementary and Alternative Medical Therapies in Conventional Medical Settings," 137 *Ann. Int. Med.* 660 (2002). The article summarizes ethical dilemmas, and also provides two hypothetical cases to reflect on the application of these factors to actual scenarios.

39. Id., at 660.

40. Id., at 663.

41. Id., at 662.

42. Id.

43. Id., at 663.

44. Id.

45. Michael H. Cohen, *Future Medicine: Ethical Dilemmas, Regulatory Challenges*, and *Therapeutic Pathways to Health Care and Healing in Human Transformation*, 50 (Ann Arbor: University of Michigan Press, 2003).

46. See, e.g., Kenneth F. Shaffner, *Assessments of Efficacy in Biomedicine: The Turn Toward Methodological Pluralism*, in Daniel Callahan, *The Role of Complementary and Alternative Medicine: Accommodating Pluralism*, 1–14 (Washington, D.C.: Georgetown University Press, 2002); Ted J. Kaptchuk, "The Double-Blind, Randomized, Placebo-Controlled Trial: Gold Standard or Gold Calf," 54 *J. Clin. Epidemiology* 541 (2001).

47. Cohen, *Future Medicine* (2003), at 53.

Chapter 2

Non-Physician CAM Practitioners

Malpractice Liability Issues

If I am a chiropractor, an acupuncturist, a massage therapist, or another non–physician practitioner of CAM therapies, am I held to malpractice standards applicable to medicine?

Each profession has its own standard of care—for example, medicine; physical therapy; nursing; chiropractic; acupuncture and traditional Oriental medicine; massage therapy. Thus, if a chiropractor is sued for malpractice, plaintiff's expert witness regarding the standard of care for chiropractic will, in most cases, be a chiropractor;[1] similarly, if an acupuncturist is sued for malpractice, plaintiff's expert witness most likely will be another acupuncturist.[2]

As mentioned, current data suggest that CAM practitioners do not get sued very often, at least relative to physicians. The major categories of claims against chiropractors have included injury to disk, failure to diagnose, fracture, aggravation of existing condition, and cerebral vascular injury; major categories of claims against massage therapists have included soft tissue injuries, fractures, sexual misconduct, and in a tiny percentage of claims, grave injuries.[3] CAM practitioners do have a duty to refer their patients to licensed medical doctors whenever the patient's condition exceeds the scope of their training, education, and competence; violation of the duty can lead to malpractice liability.[4]

As in medicine, if a key, CAM professional association publishes clinical guidelines for the profession concerning treatment under specified clinical circumstances, then failure to comply with such guidelines potentially can be evidence of negligence. Again, if the plaintiff offers evidence of negligence—whether through expert opinion, or introduction of such a clinical practice guideline—it is defendant's responsibility to introduce countervailing evidence, so as to persuade the jury that the standard of care was met.

The notable exception to the rule, that defendant health care practitioners are judged by the standards of their own professions, occurs when the CAM practitioner has offered the patient a treatment that extends into medical treatment or knowledge. In such case, plaintiff may introduce a medical expert to testify that defendant failed to meet a medical standard of care. This might occur if, for example, a chiropractor ordered x-rays or blood and other laboratory tests and used these in ways analogous to those of medical personnel; or, alternatively, if the chiropractor purported to use spinal manipulation to cure diabetes.[5]

Particularly in integrative care settings, CAM practitioners can try to limit their own potential liability for direct negligence in at least two ways: first, by referring their patients to licensed medical doctors where appropriate; and second, by suggesting to patients when appropriate that M.D.'s should administer treatments that may overlap with the CAM therapy, but particularly draw on medical expertise.

Disciplinary Issues;
Unlicensed Medical Practice

When *do I risk professional discipline?*

As in medicine, unlike malpractice (which involves a civil claim by a private party (the patient) against the practitioner), professional discipline against a CAM practitioner involves an administrative hearing by a professional regulatory board (for example, the state board of chiropractors). Although, as noted, there may be overlap between the two actions (for example, a common allegation of malpractice), they are brought by different actors (e.g., the patient in one case; a regulatory board in another) and for different purposes (e.g., to gain monetary compensation in one case, and to evaluate whether the practitioner should be sanctioned in another).

CAM regulatory boards can impose sanctions similar to the ones medical boards can impose on their licensees, the most serious being the stripping away of a practitioner's license. One of the most common scenarios, as reported in judicial opinions, involves a CAM practitioner's conduct exceeding the legislatively authorized scope of practice.

The term "scope of practice" refers to the services that licensed, non-physicians are authorized to provide by their own licensing statutes, which are narrower than the broad authority granted to physicians to "diagnose" and "treat" disease. For example, licensed chiropractors typically are authorized to use spinal manipulation and adjustment to readjust the flow of "nerve energy" in their patients; licensed acupuncturists, to use techniques of traditional oriental medicine to help adjust the "flow and balance of energy in the body," and licensed massage therapists to use "rubbing, stroking, kneading, or tapping" the muscles to promote relaxation and affect well-being.[6]

Courts (and even many CAM regulatory boards) have tended to interpret a CAM practitioner's scope of practice narrowly, just as courts historically have tended to interpret the practice of "medicine" broadly and inclusively. Thus, individual chiropractors, for example, have been disciplined by their regulatory boards in some states for recommending and selling dietary supplements to their patients, despite licensing statutes authorizing the rendering of dietary advice.[7]

A CAM practitioner who exceeds the legislatively authorized scope of practice is subject not only to potential discipline by his or her regulatory board, but also to prosecution for unlicensed medical practice. Again, this goes back to the broad, statutory definitions of "medicine" and a long history of cases interpreting such definitions sufficiently broadly to bring many different kinds of conduct, by both licensed and non-licensed practition-ers, within the statutory language. One useful strategy for clini-cians, in cases involving novel or controversial therapies, is to have professional associations (including their legal counsel, if available) check with the applicable regulatory board and state district attorney to see whether such therapies raise any "red flags" in terms of potential liability or discipline.

Yet another arena in which to be mindful is advertising. The chiropractor, acupuncturist, or other health care practitioner who makes claims of superior treatment, or exaggerates available services, may find that the standard of care against which his or her conduct is measured may be heightened by the advertising.[8] Likewise, the practitioner who guarantees the patient a cure may have invited a lawsuit for breach of contract as well as negligence.[9] With these warnings in mind, liability risk management "need not be a grudging accession to the threat of suit," but rather "should be one of many means" by which the CAM practitioner improves clinical practice and enhances patient care.[10]

The Informed Consent Obligation

What is my informed consent obligation?

Based on the patient's right to information regarding treat-ment decisions involving his or her body, the informed consent obligation arguably applies across the board, whether the practi-tioner is a physician, or a non-physician conventional health care professional (such as a nurse or psychologist), or a CAM practi-tioner.

Essentially, the practitioner should disclose all information material to a treatment decision.[11] The health care professional using CAM therapies, whether a conventional or CAM practi-tioner, should disclose and discuss the limitations of the CAM therapies suggested, and inform the patient as to whether the patient's condition is beyond the scope of the practitioner's skill and training, and whether referral to a medical doctor for the patient's condition is warranted. As noted earlier, good communication between practitioner and patient helps reduce the risk of a malpractice lawsuit, be it a lawsuit based on allegations of negligent care or one based on allegations of inadequate informed consent.

The legal obligation of informed consent often is codified in a statute, and thus presents a patchwork across states. But even if the statute (or relevant case law) imposes a reasonable standard for disclosure (based on the materiality requirement), practitioners may further reduce liability risk by going well beyond the legal requirement, and engaging patients in full and frank conversations—conversations that make patients partners, rather than dependents, in therapeutic decision-making. Such a style empowers the patient, may have therapeutic value, and keeps the practitioner clear of subtle temptations to abuse the healer's authority over the patient by withholding information or infringing on the patient's autonomy interest.[12] In short, in the arena of informed consent, legal obligations may represent a minimum rather than the ideal.

Potential Liability in Integrative Care

To what extent do I share liability with a medical doctor or another practitioner, if we are practicing "integrative" care?

As noted earlier, although cases have not yet fully developed in this area, there seems to be a trend toward increasing imposition of shared liability between and among practitioners even in conventional medical settings. As a practical matter, where a patient believes the integrative treatment caused injury, the patient or his or her family may be likely to sue each practitioner, up and down the chain of health care services. As an example, where a chiropractor and an orthopedic surgeon co-manage the patient, the two are likely to be viewed as agents for one another.

In other words, if injury results after treatment by the combination of practitioners, the chiropractor is likely to be included in a lawsuit based on the surgeon's alleged negligence; and the surgeon may be a defendant in a lawsuit arising out of a chiropractor's alleged negligence.[13] Once named, even if ultimately there is no liability, it may take some time (and legal expense) to extricate oneself from such a lawsuit.

The possibility of shared liability suggests the necessity of even greater communication between conventional and CAM practitioners than in conventional care alone. Integrative care involves team building and team maintenance, with all its associated dynamics. In this respect, potential liability follows "the logic of clinical integration," since the premise of integrative care is shared clinical responsibility for the patient's health, in a multi-disciplinary, 'team' approach to healing and cure.[14]

References for Chapter 2

1. Studdert et al. (1998), at 1614 (citing cases). Where CAM providers are unlicensed, courts may hold them to a medical standard of care.

2. Cohen (1998), at 64.

3. Studdert (1998), at 1612.

4. Cohen (1998), at 68–69 (citing cases).

5. Id., at 67 (citing cases).

6. Id., at 40–44 (citing statutes).

7. Id., at 47–49 (citing cases).

8. Michael H. Cohen, Forward, in L. K. Campbell, C. J. Ladenheim, R.P. Sherman, and L. Sportelli, *Professional Chiropractic Practice: Ethics, Business, Jurisprudence & Risk Management*, 5–8 Fincastle, Virginia: Health Services Publication (2001) (citing the text).

9. Id.

10. Id.

11. See Chapter 1 for a discussion of materiality.

12. See generally Howard Brody, *The Healer's Power*, (Yale University Press, 1993).

13. Cohen (Forward, 2001).

14. Id., at viii. "Successful collaborative efforts rely on mutual respect, humility, and a spirit of inquiry in the context of close, collegial, working rela-

tionships . . . Transformative integration patterns are the most variable . . . Moving beyond the divisions of alternative and orthodox, these patterns offer the greatest promise for the reinvention of health services and long-term strategic positioning." David C. Kailin, *Initial Strategies*, in Nancy Faass, *Integrating Complementary Medicine Into Health Systems*, 44, 46 (Gaithersburg, MD: Aspen Publishers, Inc, 2001).

Part Two: Hospitals

Hospitals and other health care institutions (such as elder care facilities), as well as managed care organizations (HMO's, PPO's, and other kinds of health plans) increasingly are being asked by patients—as well as by physicians and other health care providers within the institution—whether the institution can or should be furnishing CAM therapies or information about such therapies, and how providers should respond to requests from patients for therapeutic recommendations or information.

Some hospitals have attempted to ignore such requests, but there are potential liability implications either way. The old paradigm of ignoring or simply refusing to respond, is yielding to an interest by hospital administrators and health care executives in understanding how to respond to patient and practitioner interest in a balanced way that is sensitive to legal and ethical, as well as clinical, considerations.

Common questions include:

◆ *What is the institution's potential liability for allowing physicians and allied health professionals to offer CAM therapies to patients?*

◆ *How can institutions manage their potential malpractice liability related to offering CAM services?*

◆ *If the institution decides to allow physicians and allied health professionals to offer CAM therapies, how can the institution structure the credentialing process and make appropriate decisions?*

◆ *Aren't dietary supplements unregulated? How does this affect the institution's ability to handle patient use of dietary supplements?*

◆ *How can the institution best handle patient requests for (and sometimes, reliance on use of) dietary supplements?*

Chapters 3 through 5 address these questions.

Chapter 3

Institutional Malpractice Liability

Sources of Potential Liability

What is the institution's potential liability for allowing physicians and allied health professionals to offer CAM therapies to patients?

Hospitals and other health care institutions can be liable in malpractice on two theories: direct liability and vicarious liability. Direct liability, which is also known as corporate negligence, means that the institution has been directly negligent to the patient. In other words, the health care institution either has done something careless to injure the patient, or has carelessly neglected to do something that it should have done; and as a result, the patient has been injured.

Vicarious liability means that the institution has not necessarily done or failed to do something, but rather, becomes liable for the acts of its agents. The law imputes the agent's negligence to the health care institution, the theory being that the hospital is responsible for the agent's conduct.[1]

Typically, for example, hospital employees are considered agents of the hospital, and their negligence can be imputed to the hospital. In this way, a single negligent action can give rise to potential liability on both theories of liability: if, for example, a nurse failed to check a patient's vital signs with sufficient regularity in the intensive care unit, and the patient died as a result, plaintiff might argue that the hospital was directly negligent for failing to supervise the nurse, and vicariously negligent for the negligence of its employee.

These two theories of liability can apply regardless of whether the institution is offering conventional or CAM therapies, and regardless of whether the provider involved is a conventional or a CAM practitioner. The same principles apply across the board.

Institutions are the ultimate "deep pockets" for injured patients and thus would benefit from careful consideration of strategy in integrating CAM therapies. Many of the liability and liability management concepts articulated in Part One also are likely to translate to the institution. For example, since data to date show that there are fewer legal claims against CAM practitioners than against medical doctors, there may (for now) be fewer such claims against an institution employing CAM practitioners. The risk assessment framework presented in Part One offers health care institutions one possible basis for drafting policies about the kinds of therapies they wish to allow (or disallow), and for guiding their conventional health care professionals regarding clinical decision–making and liability assessment involving CAM therapies.

Managing Potential Liability

How can institutions manage their potential malpractice liability related to offering CAM services?

In the conventional domain, direct negligence can include failure to supervise practitioners (as suggested in the earlier hypothetical), and, as well, failure to take sufficient quality assurance measures to ensure that practitioners within the institution are reasonably competent. Again, this translates into the CAM domain. Institutions should ensure that practitioners who require supervision under state law indeed have the requisite supervision. Institutions also have a duty to take reasonable steps to ensure patient safety and well being, using methods additional to ensuring appropriate supervision of practitioners; the duty includes maintaining safe and adequate facilities and equipment, and implementing rules and policies to ensure quality care.[2]

40

In the integrative care setting, regular team meetings may help ensure that conventional and CAM practitioners can share a common language, and sufficiently communicate about different diagnostic and therapeutic techniques so that the patient is receiving due care. Further, the medical director or hospital administrator should ensure that whatever the system for patient flow, patients do receive conventional diagnostic monitoring and care as necessary.

Vicarious liability may be more difficult to manage. Conceivably, the health care institution (or managed care organization)[3] could find itself vicariously liable for the negligence of an employee CAM practitioner who either utilizes a therapy that is contraindicated for the patient or condition in question or otherwise acts negligently. Suppose, for example, that an employee of the hospital who is a chiropractor uses excessive force on a patient; or that an acupuncturist who is employed by the hospital uses a needle that is not sterile, and each thereby injures the patient; in such cases, the institution may find itself vicariously liable.

One way to avoid such scenarios is to have strong credentialing criteria in place (see next section) to ensure that practitioners are qualified and highly competent. Another is to determine what modalities, within a given CAM profession, present excessive risk, and impose institutional limitations on the practitioner's legislatively authorized scope of practice.[4] The latter may be controversial if, for example, the scope of practice includes modalities (such as herbal therapy by acupuncturists) that are intrinsic to the profession, yet not readily understood by physicians, or that are widely used within the profession yet presently lacking in satisfactory mechanistic explanations.

Still another liability management strategy is to have policies and procedures to help ensure safety. For example, an institution may have a policy to ensure disposal of used acupuncture needles as a potential biohazard. Presumably, CAM practitioners, if hired as employees, will be bound to the many administrative and other policies and procedures of the hospital. This may include such simple, public health measures as, for example, washing hands between clients, and a variety of other requirements for hospital clinicians and employees. The health care institution may need to implement some of these measures by written agreement with CAM practitioners who remain independent contractors. Simply denying patients the ability to access CAM therapies offers no easy solutions.[5] Rather, careful considerations of legal as well as economic issues can help health care institutions with the strategic planning necessary to ensure viable integration of CAM therapies and practitioners.[6]

References for Chapter 3

1. See Alan Dumoff, "Malpractice Liability of Alternative/Complementary Health Care Providers: A View From the Trenches," 1(4) *Alt. & Comp. Therapies* 248 and 1(5) Alt. & Comp. Therapies 333 (1995).

2. Cohen (1998), at 68–72 (citing cases).

3. See Alan Dumoff, "Including Alternative Providers in Managed Care: Managing the Malpractice Risk (Part I & II)," *Medical Interface* (May & June, 1995).

4. See Michael H. Cohen and David M. Eisenberg, "Potential Physician Malpractice Liability Associated With Complementary/Integrative Medical Therapies," 136 *Ann. Int. Med.* 596, 597 (2002); David M. Eisenberg, Michael H. Cohen, Andrea Hrbek, Jonathon Grayzel, Maria Van Rompay, and Richard M. Cooper, "Credentialing Complementary and Alternative Medical Providers," 137 *Ann. Int. Med.* 965 (2002).

5. See P. C. Walker, "Evolution of a Policy Disallowing the Use of Alternative Therapies in a Health System," 57:21 *Am. J. Health Pol.* 1984 (2000).

6. See Faass (2001), 41–114 (discussing practical aspects of strategic planning within the health care institution considering integration of CAM therapies).

Chapter 4

Credentialing

Physicians and Allied Health Professionals

I*f the institution decides to allow physicians and allied health professionals to offer CAM therapies, how can the institution structure the credentialing process and make appropriate decisions?*

The Joint Commission on Accreditation of Healthcare Organizations (JCAHO) has a number of rules by which hospitals must abide, governing matters such as credentialing and privileging. These rules should be considered when credentialing various practitioners and granting clinical privileges to them to deliver CAM therapies.

Institutions and practitioners often confuse credentialing and privileging. According to JCAHO, credentialing, also known as credentials review, means: "the process of obtaining, verifying, and assessing the qualifications of a health care practitioner to provide patient care services in or for a health care organization."[1] Privileging, or giving a practitioner clinical privileges, means: "the process whereby the specific scope and content of patient care services (that is, clinical privileges) are authorized for a health care practitioner by a health care organization based on evaluation of the individual's credentials and performance."[2]

According to JCAHO's Comprehensive Accreditation Manual for Hospitals: "All individuals who are permitted by law and by the hospital to provide patient care services independently in the hospital must have delineated clinical privileges, whether or not they are medical staff members."[3] In other words, practitioners who deliver patient care services independent of medical supervision, and are permitted by their licensing statutes (as well as by hospital rules) to do so, must receive formal clinical privileges. Such privileges typically spell out what procedures the practitioner may perform. Hospitals have a rigorous internal process to verify the credentials of such practitioners and ensure that they are qualified and competent to offer such procedures.

Practitioners who practice dependently (i.e., under the supervision of M.D.'s or D.O.'s), typically go through a similar, but often less rigorous credentialing process, generally outside of the medical staff office and through either their own departments (e.g., physical therapy; nutrition; exercise physiology), or, the hospital's Human Resources department. This credentialing process occurs according to established policies and procedures that help the relevant department (or Human Resources) evaluate such matters as training and current competence, media requirements for licensure, and compliance with applicable laws.[4]

Formal clinical privileges, once granted, usually cannot be taken away arbitrarily, as their deprivation is subject to Due Process rules; and practitioners who are members of the medical staff also have contractual rights (such as the ability to admit patients to the hospital) and obligations that are delineated in the medical staff bylaws.

In addition to structuring credentialing and privileging decisions, the institution may have other rules applicable to introduction of CAM therapies. For example, there may be a rule requiring hospital practitioners to submit any "new" (CAM) therapies they propose to use through relevant hospital committees (such as, for example, a medication use committee if dietary supplements are involved; and potentially the hospital's Institutional Review Board). Yet another arena of concern is scope of practice. Institutions should investigate whether practitioners' own regulatory boards impose any conditions or limitations on use of CAM therapies. For instance, nursing boards in a number of states have addressed the use of CAM therapies as part of legislatively authorized scope of nursing practice.

Institutions, like individual physicians, also should pay attention to the model guidelines promulgated by the Federation of State Medical Boards, which aim to govern the practice of CAM therapies by physicians, and particularly address issues of deciding what therapies to offer and how to document use of these treatments. As suggested, these guidelines, while they express model rules and have not necessarily been adopted by each state, may exercise influence on the medical board, particularly if other regulation in the relevant state is lacking.[5]

CAM Practitioners

I*f the institution decides to include CAM therapies and/or practitioners, how can it structure the credentialing process and make appropriate hiring decisions?*

Credentialing CAM practitioners generally is no different than credentialing physicians and allied health professionals.[6] The essential steps include verification of: valid, current state licensure; evidence of satisfactory completion of an appropriate national certification examination; documentation of completion of required studies and continuing education; signed statements pertaining to a specified minimum amount of malpractice insurance; documentation of history of malpractice litigation; and documentation of disciplinary action.[7]

The latter two are intended to help the institution determine the extent to which the practitioner is a liability risk. Institutions may wish to set standards to help decide whether a certain level or kind of claim (in either the malpractice or disciplinary arena) will be sufficient to prevent hiring a given candidate. For example, allegations of negligence that have been dismissed by a judge well before trial, might be viewed differently than claims that have been aired at a hearing before a professional regulatory board involving allegations of sexual abuse.

Beyond these minimum requirements, institutions seeking a higher level of quality assurance can add criteria such as: a pre-established minimum number of years in practice; assessment of practice demographics; letters of recommendation from M.D.'s, D.O.'s and other conventional practitioners to help evaluate how (or how well) the practitioner has co-managed patients; and assessment through site visits.[8]

Checking the CAM practitioner's credentials, as outlined above, can give the institution some comfort in authorizing the practitioner to deliver clinical services to patients. This process, however, typically authorizes these practitioners to treat outpatients (often within an integrative care setting), since inpatient care involves greater degrees of coordination with conventional caregivers, and may be politically sensitive, and/or be authorized on a case-by-case basiswith specified classes of patients.

The process of getting the institution to agree in the first place to credential CAM practitioners, and to generate consensus mechanisms to credential such practitioners, raises different questions. These questions vary by institution, as local politics and preferences regarding CAM therapies vary.

Strategies to gain institutional acceptance might include: gradual educational and public relations efforts within institutions; building on existing credentialing processes for allied health professionals; reviewing national standards for practitioners lacking licensure (for example, yoga therapists); involving key players within the institution, including key skeptics and critics, in the process; drawing on existing models within the human resources department; and carefully negotiating authorized scope of practice.[9]

References for Chapter 4

1. *Credentials Review and Privileging: Questions and Answers for Ambulatory Care*, JCAHO, 1999.

2. Id.

3. MS.5.14 (JCAHO).

4. JCAHO (1999).

5. The guidelines have, in fact, already been subject to legal challenge, http://www.apma.net/misc/FSMBletter.doc.

6. http://www.credentialinfo.com.

7. Eisenberg et al. (2002). Hospitals can use various national databases to discover whether practitioners have been disciplined. A major database is the National Practitioner Databank, a national register of physicians, dentists, and other health care practitioners, established by the federal government. The NPDB "gathers information about practitioners' professional competence and conduct from different regulating organizations for release to eligible entities. NPDB information includes adverse actions against practitioners' clinical privileges, licensure, and professional society memberships. It also gives information about medical malpractice payments." This and related information can be found at http://www.credentialinfo.com/cred/dbintros/databank/npdb.cfm. The chiropractic profession has its own interjurisdictional chiropractic board action database, called CIN-BAD, which is run by the Federation of Chiropractic Licensing Boards, http://www.flcb.org.

8. Eisenberg et al. (2002).

9. Michael H. Cohen and Mary C. Ruggie, "Integrating Complementary and Alternative Medical Therapies in Conventional Medical Settings: Legal Quandaries and Potential Policy Models," Cinn. L. Rev., 2004 72:2:671-729. Michael H. Cohen and Mary C. Ruggie, "Overcoming Legal and Social Barriers to Integrative Medicine, Medical Law Intl 2004:6:339-393. These law review articles summarize and analyze interviews of key personnel in integrative care centers, in a project funded by the National Library of Medicine, National Institutes of Health.

Chapter 5

Dietary Supplement Policies

Regulation of Dietary Supplements

A*ren't dietary supplements unregulated? How does this affect the institution's ability to handle patient use of dietary supplements?*

The regulatory category of "dietary supplements" causes institutions (and clinicians) considerable confusion, both clinically and legally. A key to clarifying the legal issues is understanding the Dietary Supplements Health Education Act of 1994 (DSHEA).[1] This statute, enacted because of overwhelming consumer interest in making vitamins, minerals, herbs, and other substances more freely available, changed the way the federal Food and Drug Administration (FDA) regulated these substances.

Essentially, DSHEA affirmed that dietary supplements were to be regulated as "foods," and not "drugs." This means that as a general proposition, so long as they do not make impermissible claims linking their products to treatment or cure of disease, manufacturers of dietary supplements do not have to prove safety and efficacy prior to marketing and distributing dietary supplements interstate.

The legal definition of a dietary supplement is: "a product (other than tobacco) intended to supplement the diet that bears or contains one or more of the following ingredients: (A) a vitamin; (B) a mineral; (C) an herb or botanical; (D) amino acids; (E) a dietary substance for use by man to supplement the diet by increasing the total dietary intake; or (F) a concentrate, metabolite, constituent, extract, or any combination of any ingredient described in clause (A), (B), (C), (D), or (E)."[2] Three of the most popular substances meeting this definition are Echinacea, gingko, and St. John's Wort. These dietary supplements can be found on the shelves of most pharmacies, as well as health food stores.

Manufacturers do not need to register themselves nor their dietary supplement products with FDA before producing or selling them. At present, no FDA regulations specific to dietary supplements establish minimum manufacturing standards, although the FDA is issuing regulations on good manufacturing practices, to help ensure the identity, purity, quality, strength and composition of dietary supplements.[3]

Many people make the mistake of thinking that DSHEA leaves dietary supplements unregulated. This is untrue. It is true that because of DSHEA, the extensive, pre-marketing testing requirements required for new "drugs" do not apply to "dietary supplements." However, under DSHEA, a dietary supplement is considered unlawfully "adulterated," if it presents a "significant or unreasonable risk of illness or injury" when used as directed on the label, or under normal conditions of use.

In addition, the Secretary of the Department of Health and Human Services (DHHS) has authority to remove from the market a dietary supplement that poses an imminent hazard to public health or safety. But, whereas with new drugs, the manufacturer has the burden of proving safety and efficacy, with dietary supplements, the U.S. government has the burden of proving that the product is unsafe and must be taken off the shelves.

One important aspect of regulation under DSHEA concerns the labeling of dietary supplements. Under federal law, "labeling" includes what goes on the packaging, inserts, and the promotional material distributed at the point of sale. With passage of DSHEA, there now are several kinds of claims a manufacturer can make in labeling a dietary supplement, the most common being a "disease claim," a "health claim," a "structure–function claim," a "general well–being claim," and a "nutrient claim."

Briefly, a "disease claim" suggests that the dietary supplement is intended to diagnose, treat, mitigate, cure, or prevent a specific disease (for example, stating that a product treats depression). A "health claim" characterizes the relationship between the product and a disease or health-related condition (for example, the relationship between calcium and osteoporosis).

One important innovation DSHEA established was the "structure-function claim." This kind of claim characterizes the documented mechanisms by which the product acts to maintain the structure or a function of the body (for example, "fiber maintains bowel regularity;" or "calcium maintains strong bones"). The "structure-function claim" is quite common among dietary supplements, and allows manufacturers to make a statement linking the dietary supplement to health, without violating the prohibition against making "disease claims."

Related to this is the "general well-being claim," which describes the general well-being that a consumer might expect from consuming the product. A "nutrient claim" describes a benefit related to a classical nutrient deficiency disease (for example, vitamin C and scurvy).

There are various legal requirements for each kind of claim. For example, a "health claim" must be pre-approved by the FDA before it goes on the label, and must be supported by "significant scientific agreement" among "qualified scientists," that the "claimed link" between the product and the disease is valid.

A "structure-function claim" must have scientific substantiation that the statement is truthful and not misleading. Further, such a claim must be accompanied by a disclaimer, which alerts the consumer that the FDA has not evaluated the claim, and that the product is not intended to "diagnose, treat, cure, or prevent any disease." Unlike the "health claim," the "structure-function claim" need not be pre-approved by the FDA. But again, if a dietary supplement does contain a "disease claim" on its label, the product is subject to regulation as a drug, which means the manufacturer must show safety and efficacy prior to interstate marketing and distribution.

In actual practice, it may be difficult for the consumer (or clinician, or health care institution trying to set policy) to distinguish the different kinds of claims. It is hard to tell, for example, why a claim such as "for the relief of occasional sleeplessness" would be acceptable, but a claim with similar language, such as "helps you fall asleep if you have difficulty falling asleep" would be unacceptable. According to the FDA regulations, the latter is a "disease claim," implying that the product treats a disease or condition, insomnia, while the former is "structure–function claim." The lines between the two, though, are difficult to distinguish.

Moreover, increasingly, companies are blurring the boundaries of these different kinds of claims, by manufacturing and marketing what they call "nutraceuticals." This is not a regulatory term, but an industry term used to describe and sell these products. The term nutraceuticals, which sounds like pharmaceuticals, is designed to imply that the product both is nutritious, and contains properties that support health. The category includes medical foods, dietary supplements, and what are now called "functional foods"—foods that incorporate dietary supplements. For example, a company might sell potato chips and pretzels that contain St. John's Wort or gingko.

It probably would be difficult for anyone without specialized knowledge about botanicals to understand whether such "dietary supplements," when added to foods, have any clinically therapeutic effect. Nonetheless, present legal rules would allow marketing of such "nutraceuticals" without prior FDA approval of the claim on the label (so long as the claim falls within the acceptable parameters described above).

All of this complicates attempts by health care institutions to respond to patient requests concerning dietary supplements, and to help clinicians decide how to address such requests. The above description of the regulatory landscape aims to provide some clarity around relevant legal rules so that clinicians can better inform patients about the meaning of statements on the labels of the dietary supplements. Informed clinicians also can better advise patients as to risks and what relevance the claims on the label may have, if any, to potential therapeutic benefit.

In addition, institutions and clinicians—as well as patients—can alert themselves to the distinctions federal regulations draw between "disease claims" and the various therapeutic claims authorized by FDA rules that steer clear from linking products to treatment of disease. As suggested, the difference between the different claims can often seem like semantics. Certainly, such distinctions can produce artful drafting by attorneys with expertise in food and drug law. Although the regulatory guidelines attempt to defend a conceptual distinction between maintaining wellness and treating disease, the lines in actual practice are probably more blurred.[4]

As a final note, the FDA, a federal agency, has no jurisdiction over the practice of medicine, which is a matter of state and not federal law. This means that presumably, the FDA has no jurisdiction over what is said between practitioner and patient concerning dietary supplements. Nonetheless, each state has its own version of the federal laws that the FDA enforces.

Further, other state regulatory agencies may intervene if practitioners make excessive claims regarding dietary supplements or subject their patients to harm by recommending such supplements. Some states regulate potential conflicts of interest by putting limits (or prohibitions) on practitioners' sales of dietary supplements; in addition, some federal as well as many state laws prohibit certain kinds of financial arrangements between practitioners and clinics in which they have a financial interest.[5] Professional organizations such as the American Medical Association may offer their own ethical opinions regarding such practices. All these rules require careful attention by legal counsel familiar with the practitioner's precise situation.

Responding to Patient Use

How can the institution best handle patient requests for (and sometimes, reliance on use of) dietary supplements?

Some professional organizations are now beginning to implement guidelines governing patient use of dietary supplements in conventional medical settings. For example, recently, the American Society of Anesthesiologists issued a recommendation that: "(1) surgical patients taking herbal medications stop taking these products at least two weeks prior to elective surgery if possible; (2) prior to surgery, patients consult their doctors regarding dietary supplements; (3) patients who have questions about potential herb–drug interactions should contact their primary care doctor." Interestingly, the Society has assumed that primary care doctors have (or should have) knowledge concerning the dietary supplements patients might use and potentially relevant herb-drug interactions.

The Society cautioned that: "use of herbal medications is not necessarily a contraindication for anesthesia." In other words, the recommendation did not necessarily disallow surgical patients from using dietary supplements.

The Society also issued a disclaimer that its suggestions were meant to enhance patient safety, but could not guarantee a specific outcome. The Society thus mixed a quasi–legal caveat in its clinical guidance. Clearly, clinicians and institutions would benefit from staying abreast of similar, current developments in relevant professional organizations.

Further, clinicians within institutions could follow the informed consent suggestions offered earlier. For example, clinicians may wish to counsel their patients regarding: (1) known toxicities and adverse events associated with a particular dietary supplement the patient is currently taking; (2) any medical evidence relevant to safety and efficacy (or lack thereof), as well as the documented mechanism of action; (3) the fact that anecdotal reports concerning the dietary supplement's effectiveness do not constitute medical proof of efficacy.[6]

Moreover, clinicians (in addition to pharmacists) should be mindful of the distinctions made by federal regulations about the different kinds of labeling claims. Most non-physicians, as noted, are not allowed to prescribe drugs. And although dietary supplements are in a different regulatory category under federal food and drug law, cases—as described in Part One—have been brought against non-physician clinicians who have recommended dietary supplements, on the theory that these clinicians have prescribed "drugs."

Furthermore, as noted, it may be troubling that federal law treats a dietary supplement with a "disease claim" as a "drug." Non-physician clinicians who use dietary supplements to help treat disease could, in a worst-case scenario, be viewed as having crossed the line into practicing "medicine" unlawfully. It may therefore be wise for clinicians (and pharmacists) to limit claims about the therapeutic benefits of dietary supplements to what is stated on the label. This caution should not, of course, prevent honest conversations about potential clinical risks and benefits, and disclosure and discussion about what may be unknown about the products (and their potential interaction with other therapeutic agents) as well as what is known.

Clinicians and institutions also should be aware of laws and regulations, if any, within their own state, governing recommendations concerning, and sales of, dietary supplements. For example, in addition to the legislative scope of practice limitations discussed in Part One for various CAM practitioners such as chiropractors, and related to giving patients dietary and nutritional advice, some states have rules governing clinicians' sales of dietary supplements.

Some of these rules apply equally to dietary supplements and pharmaceutical drugs. For instance, New Jersey provides: "A physician shall not dispense more than a seven-day supply of drugs or medicines to any patient. The drugs or medicines shall be dispensed at or below . . . cost . . . plus . . . 10%."[7]

Health care institutions also have to decide how to handle patient use of dietary supplements, particularly in the inpatient setting, even apart from use during surgery and scope of practice. As a starting point, institutions must decide whether to have a formal, written policy regarding dietary supplements, or simply have an informational resource (such as a library, a knowledgeable person within the hospital pharmacy, or a Web site) within the institution, to respond to practitioner requests and, if appropriate, help initiate educational courses for clinicians.

The next step is to decide whether to include dietary supplements in the outpatient or inpatient formulary, and if so, what criteria to use to decide what products and brands to stock. Commonly used supplements, such as Echinacea and St. John's Wort, might be more acceptable than unfamiliar herbs. Manufacturers of certain brands may have a better reputation for quality control and good manufacturing practices than others.

A related issue is whether to confiscate dietary supplements during patient admission, or establish criteria to determine which dietary supplement products patients might continue using, from their home supply, during hospitalization. These decisions are likely to require legal as well as clinical input, and to involve multiple decision makers within the institution to fashion a policy that responds to patient interests, while honoring clinical sensibilities.[8]

References for Chapter 5

1. *Dietary Supplements Health Education Act*, 103 P.L. 417; 108 Stat. 4325; 1994.

2. Pub. L. No. 103-417, 108 Stat. 4325, 21 U.S.C. § § 301 et seq. (1994).

3. U. S. Food and Drug Administration, Center for Food Safety and Applied Nutrition, *Overview of Dietary Supplements*, http://vm.cfsan.fda.gov/-~dms/ds-oview.html). The FDA's recent, proposed rule regarding good manufacturing practices for dietary supplements, http://www.fda.gov/-bbs/topics/NEWS/dietarysupp.

4. See Alan Dumoff, "Defining Disease: The Latest Struggle for Turf in Dietary Supplement Regulation," 6 (2) *Alt. & Comp. Therapies* 95 (2000).

5. Alan Dumoff has written a number of helpful articles in this arena. See Alan Dumoff, "State Medical Board Prohibitions on Physician Sale of Supplements: A Looming Issue Physician Consult," (Aug. 2000); Alan Dumoff, "Medical Board Prohibitions Against Physician Supplements Sales," 6(4) *Alt. & Comp. Therapies* 226 (2000). As suggested, other rules, such as those prohibiting so-called "kickbacks" and "self-referrals," also may apply. See generally Alan Dumoff, "Regulating Professional Relationships: Kickback and Self-Referral Restrictions on Collaborative Practice," 6(1) *Alt. & Comp. Therapies* 41 (2000); see also Alan Dumoff, "Understanding the Kassenbaum–Kennedy Health Care Act: Addressing Legitimate Concerns and Irrational Fears," 3(4) *Alt. & Comp. Therapies* 309; Alan C. Dumoff, "Legislation versus Self-Regulation in the Somatic Practices Field: Comments from the Editor," 3(3) *Alt. & Comp. Therapies* 220 (1997). See also L. K. Campbell, C. J. Ladenheim, R. P. Sherman, and L. Sportelli, *Professional Chiropractic Practice: Ethics, Business, Jurisprudence & Risk Management*, 53–90, 157–213, Fincastle, Virginia: Health Services Publication (2001) (discussing broader legal concerns applicable to CAM practitioners such as chiropractors).

6. Some of the suggestions and material in this chapter were given as part of a talk, entitled, Michael H. Cohen, "Regulatory and Legal Issues Concerning Herbal Therapies and Dietary Supplements," at a conference entitled, "Herbal Therapies and Other Dietary Supplements: What the Practicing Physician, Pharmacist or Nurse Needs to Know" (sponsored by Harvard Medical School and the University of California, San Francisco).

7. N.J. Bd. Of Med. Examiners, Regulation 45.9-22.11.

8. Michael H. Cohen, A. Hrbek, R. Davis, S. Schachter and M. Eisenberg, "Emerging Credentialing Practices, Malpractice Liability Policies, and Guidlines Governing Complementary and Alternative Medical Practices and Dietary Supplements Recommendations: A Descriptive Study of 19 Integrative Health Care Centers in the U.S.," *Arch. Int. Med.* (2004)

Part Three: Patients

Patients, both in hospital, and as regular consumers of CAM therapies in daily life, often ask the following questions:

- *In general, do I have a right to access CAM therapies and practitioners?*

- *If I want a non–FDA approved treatment that may be life saving, under what circumstances can I get it?*

- *What CAM therapies am I most likely to get in the hospital?*

- *How can I get my physician to talk to me about CAM therapies, and/or to offer me these therapies within the hospital setting?*

- *Is it legally safe to provide CAM therapies to my child who is ill?*

- *How broadly are CAM therapies such as massage therapy and acupuncture reimbursed by health insurance?*

- *How can I get insurance reimbursement for CAM therapies such as massage therapy and acupuncture?*

Chapters 6 and 7 address these questions.

Chapter 6

Access to Treatment

Consumer Rights

I*n general, do I have a right to access CAM therapies and practitioners?*

When this nation was founded, any individual could offer health care services, irrespective of the system of medicine practiced—botanical, Native American, or the medicine of the times (which included bleeding and vomiting the patient). In the mid-1700's, medical licensing originated as a means to separate those with training from practitioners whose ignorance posed a danger to patients.

That system of licensure, together with the organization of professional medical societies, grew over two centuries into a powerful mechanism to suppress and eliminate economic rivals to biomedicine, including chiropractors, naturopathic physicians, and herbalists. The American Medical Association (AMA) was founded in large measure to eliminate practitioners of homeopathic medicine, the AMA's most popular rival, and as late as 1990, a federal court found (in *Wilk v. American Medical Association*) that the AMA had engaged in a "conspiracy to eliminate a licensed profession," namely, chiropractic.[1] The history of health care in the U.S. is rife with anticompetitive tendencies by both "regular," "conventional," "scientific" practitioners, and the "alternative" healers.

Within the context of this maelstrom, the U.S. Supreme Court decided in an early case, *Dent v. West Virginia (1888)*, that a health care practitioner had no right, under the U.S. Constitution, to offer health care services according to his or her own system of medicine, and that the practitioner's own state had

Constitutional power to determine who may receive a license to practice health care services, and who may be excluded from licensure as a danger to public health.[2]

In subsequent cases, the U.S. Supreme Court affirmed the state's broad authority, under the "police power"—the Constitutional power to protect public health, safety, welfare, and morals—to regulate health care, even over the objections of the individual practitioner or health care consumer.[3] For example, the Court rejected a patient's argument that he had the right to care for his body in whatever seemed best to him, and upheld the state's right to order compulsory vaccination for children (1904).[4]

In perhaps the most dramatic case, *U.S. v. Rutherford (1979)*, the Court rejected the argument of terminally ill cancer patients that they had a right to privacy, under the U.S. Constitution, to obtain laetrile, then a non–FDA approved drug.[5] The Court pointed to language in the federal Food, Drug, and Cosmetic Act, requiring the FDA to approve a new drug for interstate distribution only on a sufficient showing of safety and efficacy by the manufacturer. The Court noted that Congress reasonably could have intended, in enacting the statute, to authorize the FDA to shield even terminally ill patients from unsafe or ineffective drugs.

Patients may have certain rights, in hospitals, under the Patient Bill of Rights, but in general, there is no right, guaranteed under the U.S. Constitution, to the medicine or medical system of one's choice. Indeed, the medical system is largely paternalistic—following the model of physician as benevolent parent—with the respect for patient autonomy manifested in the informed consent doctrine as a notable exception.[6]

The "health freedom" statutes noted in the earlier section on professional discipline represent one major reversal of this trend.[7] In addition, a major exception to the model of paternalism as regards CAM therapies is the "right" consumers have to dietary supplements under DSHEA. This is not a Constitutional right, but rather an ability to have access to dietary supplements, without FDA approval, because of a statute passed by Congress. Consumers have this access in the marketplace since dietary supplements are regulated as foods, not drugs.

This does not, however, mean that a patient can have dietary supplements on demand within the inpatient hospital setting. On the contrary, many hospitals confiscate dietary supplements once the patient is admitted. Since the patient's medical doctor is responsible for administering proper medical care, the patient has little remedy, except to try to engage the physician in shared decision-making (see below). The FDA provides some information on safety and efficacy of dietary supplements for consumers in its websites.[8] The FDA also notes that if a patient has suffered a serious harmful effect or illness from a product FDA regulates, including dietary supplements, the first thing the patient should do is contact a healthcare provider immediately, and then report this problem to FDA.[9]

Non-FDA Approved Drugs

I*f I want a non FDA approved treatment that may be life-saving, under what circumstances can I get it?*

As suggested above, the U.S. Supreme Court has not found a Constitutional right to obtain non-FDA approved treatments. As a result, many patients (and their families) have been unable to obtain treatments they believe helpful, but which have not been proven safe and effective as new drugs.

A notable series of cases have involved patients of Dr. Stanislaw Burzynski (a physician currently residing in Texas) whose treatments for brain tumors have found many adherents among patients, despite the lack of FDA approval. Patients testified before Congress that they tried to get Dr. Burzynski's treatments to help themselves or their children or other loved ones, who were dying of brain cancer, but that the FDA blocked their access to these therapies, based on its authority under federal food and drug law.[10]

The rationale of the *Rutherford* case has consistently supported FDA authority to block access to non-FDA approved treatments. Patients can, however, access such treatments under a number of circumscribed routes, such as the "compassionate use" exemption for an IND (investigational new drug), that allow patients to receive access to life-saving, non-FDA therapies under certain circumstances. Such exemptions are granted by the FDA on a case-by-case basis, and yet still do not constitute a broad consumer right to access unapproved therapies.

Some of these exemptions are granted only if the patient is willing to participate in clinical trials as a human research subject, as specified in the relevant FDA regulations. The patient agreeing to such participation typically is asked to review and sign a detailed informed consent form, which, among other things, spells out the risks and benefits of the treatment and informs the patient that the treatment is experimental. Patients who agree to this process should understand that such a consent form generally includes a provision allowing the patient to withdraw from the trial at any time.

Access in Hospital Settings

What CAM therapies am I most likely to get in the hospital?

As noted, the consumer has no Constitutional right to the therapy of his or her choice; and similarly, inpatients in hospital settings have no right to receive CAM therapies in general, or any specific therapy.

Patients do have a kind of right, however, to disclosure by the clinician of all reasonable and feasible alternatives—all those relevant to a treatment decision—including alternatives involving CAM therapies, if clinically reasonable and feasible. This is part of the clinician's informed consent obligation described in Part One; a clinician who fails the obligation of informed consent may be liable in malpractice.

Moreover, some CAM therapies may, over time, become so generally accepted within the medical community as to become standard of care. An example might be the use of acupuncture to relieve nausea following chemotherapy treatment. A clinician who fails to provide the patient with such care could, arguably, be said to have acted negligently, and thus to be liable in malpractice.[11]

But this kind of thinking could take years to become widely accepted as a proposition of law. Therefore, patients would not be served by making threats of litigation based on these theories. An adversary posture does nothing to enhance the therapeutic alliance between practitioner and patient. A more effective strategy might be to bring up therapies in which the patient is interested, and see whether the clinician is familiar with such therapies, knows the medical literature, and can describe risks and benefits based on the evidence. For example, some dietary supplements might be helpful in managing certain aspects of the disease (for example, St. John's Wort for certain kinds of depression), but might have adverse herb-drug interactions that the physician may wish to raise and discuss with the patient. A strategy of engaging in shared decision-making may work best.

Indeed, a brief conversation might establish that some therapies are being provided within the hospital, albeit by different units in an uncoordinated fashion. The most common example would be acupuncture—which is sometimes offered by hospital anesthesia departments; another would be massage therapy, which is sometimes combined with physical therapy. The patient could inquire into the availability of such therapies within the institution, and see whether such therapies might be appropriately provided for the condition at hand.

A variety of mind-body therapies also should be available somewhere within the hospital. For example, many of the hospital's mental health care professionals should be familiar with relaxation therapies, such as visualization and guided imagery, and clinical hypnotherapy.

A variety of CAM therapies are also available for self-care (including nutritional therapies, relaxation therapies (such as visualization), and movement therapies); one can inquire whether the hospital has any educational programs focusing on self-care. Furthermore, it may be helpful to remember that CAM therapies can be provided competently and in a nurturing way not only by CAM practitioners, but also by licensed conventional providers who are properly trained in the CAM modality (e.g., massage by licensed physical therapists; reiki by licensed nurses; intuitive counseling and hypnotherapy, guided imagery, and shamanic healing by appropriately trained psychologists and psychiatrists).

Shared Decision Making

How can I get my physician to talk to me about CAM therapies, and/or to offer me these therapies within the hospital setting?

Shared decision making means using a different process than the usual, bureaucratic and perfunctory informed consent, which typically is focused largely around getting the patient to sign a form. In shared decision making, the clinician is willing to engage the patient in a conversation, in which the physician explains risks and benefits of alternative treatment plans—including risks and benefits relating to the dietary supplements about which the patient wishes to learn—and helps the patient make an informed choice.

Shared decision making is a less authoritarian and more empowering model of health care. This model engages the patient and physician as allies in the process of bringing about cure and healing. But it may be less feasible where the physician's time is constrained by managed care, as well as patient flow considerations.

Treatment of Children

Is it legally safe to provide CAM therapies to my child who is ill?

Not all CAM therapies are safe, and not all CAM therapies are safe for children. There are at least two categories of risk. The first is direct harm, which means that the therapy creates "direct toxic effects, compromising adequate nutrition, interrupting beneficial medications or therapies, or postponing biomedical therapies of proven effectiveness."[12] The second is indirect harm by creating an unwarranted financial and emotional burden.[13]

There are many case reports documenting direct or indirect harm from use of CAM therapies on children and infants. A few of the case reports in the medical literature include fatal hypomagnesemia in a child treated with megavitamin and mega mineral therapy;[14] quadriplegia after chiropractic manipulation in an infant with congenital torticollis;[15] and tumor progression in two pediatric patients using dietary supplements and shark cartilage to treat cancer.[16] This means that clinicians who read these reports may increasingly be alert to signs that parents may unwittingly be inflicting direct or indirect harm on their children through use of CAM and neglect of appropriate conventional guidance or care.

In general, therefore, in many cases, it is probably a good idea to check planned use of CAM therapies with one's pediatrician or conventional caregiver. This will help ensure that no sources of direct or indirect harm are overlooked, and that in making any diagnostic or therapeutic decisions for their children, parents are guided by a clinician with medical training and skill.

One must, of course, draw a balance between precaution and self-care. With the arrival of the Internet, it is now possible to find a great deal of information about CAM therapies without having to check with one's physician; there is definitely a trend toward increasing consumer autonomy and empowerment, and a decline in reliance on physician authority to make health care choices.

At the same time, the medical evidence regarding CAM therapies is in flux, and may or may not be accurately represented or reported in the websites consumers will access for information. Consumers could be confused, for example, by the suggestion that dietary supplements can be put into fractions for children's dosages, like pharmaceuticals. Parents also are likely to be unfamiliar with potential adverse effects of dietary supplements and other CAM products, including adverse reactions with conventional therapies, issues of contamination and misidentification of ingredients in dietary supplements, and other hazards.

In life-threatening clinical situations involving children, parents rejecting conventional care have faced prosecution for abuse and neglect (and/or child endangerment and homicide), and removal of the child from parental custody and transfer to a state authority such as the department of public welfare. In the most drastic cases, and upon clear and convincing evidence of neglect, courts have been able to terminate parental rights and allow adoption.[17] But where the child's condition has been other than life threatening, courts have been reluctant to intervene and overrule parental choice of treatment for their child.

This suggests that parents generally run less risk of legal trouble if they use CAM therapies that are relatively safe (such as, some would argue, homeopathy for recurrent ear infections), and consult with their physicians. On the other hand, if the child's condition is serious, and the parents wish to use CAM therapies, and the physician strongly disagrees, the parents could find themselves in a difficult and adverse situation with their caregiver. States have child abuse reporting statutes, which require physicians, among others, to report to law enforcement officials instances of child abuse that come to their attention through performance of official duties. Thus, if the parents insist on using CAM therapies and the child's health thereby significantly deteriorates, reporting requirements may be triggered, leading to potential intervention by an agency such as the state department of public welfare. Again, the risk should not be overstated unless a serious condition is involved, and the parents wish to use a CAM therapy instead of a conventional therapy. In this situation, it may be helpful to find a competent physician who is still mindful or risks and benefits and the need for necessary medical care, yet more understanding of options involving CAM therapy. It may also be helpful to assess the situation with legal counsel.

References for Chapter 6

1. This history is recapped in greater detail in Cohen (1998), at 15-21 (citing sources), and Ted J. Kaptchuk and David M. Eisenberg, "Varieties of Healing 1: Medical Pluralism in the United States," 135 *Ann. Int. Med.* 189 (2001).

2. 129 U.S. 114 (1888).

3. I discuss some of these cases in Cohen (1998), at 24-26.

4. Id. at 25 (citing *Jacobson v. Massachusetts*, 197 U.S. 11 (1905)).

5. 442 U.S. 544 (1979). I discuss this case in Cohen (1998), at 23, 82-83, and 105.

6. Cohen (1995), at 138 (citing sources).

7. Indeed, the language of some of the health freedom statutes assert patient right to access therapies of choice; for example, Florida allows "citizens ... to make informed choices for any type of health care they deem to be an effective option for treating human disease ... including the prevailing or conventional treatment methods as well as other treatments designed to complement or substitute." *Fla. Stat.* § 456.41.

8. The FDA includes the following sites: "Tips For The Savvy Supplement User: Making Informed Decisions And Evaluating Information," http://-www.cfsan.fda.gov/˜dms/ds-savvy.html) (includes information on how to evaluate research findings and health information online) and "Claims That Can Be Made for Conventional Foods and Dietary Supplements," http://www.cfsan.fda.gov/˜dms/hclaims.html, (this site provides information on what types of claims can be made for dietary supplements).

9. The patient may do so by calling the FDA's MedWatch hotline at 1-800-FDA-1088, or submitting a report by fax to 1-800-FDA-0178, or online at http://www.fda.gov/medwatch/report/hcp.htm. The FDA notes that the identity of the reporter and/or patient is kept confidential, and

states that for a general, not serious, complaint or concern about food products, including dietary supplements, the patient may contact the consumer complaint coordinator at the nearest local FDA District Office; telephone numbers are available online on the FDA's Web site, http://www.fda.gov/opacom/backgrounders/complain.html.

10. I discuss this at greater length in Cohen (1998), at 76–77 (citing testimony).

11. See id., at 42–44 (citing *Moore v. Baker*, 1991 U.S. Dist. LEXIS 14712, at *11 (S.D. Ga., Sept. 5, 1991), aff'd, 989 F.2d 1129 (11th Cir. 1993)).

12. American Academy of Pediatrics, "Counseling Families Who Choose Complementary and Alternative Medicine For Their Child With Chronic Illness of Disability," 107 *Pediatrics* 598–601 (2001).

13. Id.

14. J. K. McGuire, M. S. Kulkarni, and H. P. Baden, "Fatal Hypermagnesemia in a Child Treated With Megavitamin/Megamineral Therapy," 105(2) *Pediatrics* E18 (2000).

15. Y. Shafrir and B. A. Kaufman, "Quadriplegia After Chiropractic Manipulation in an Infant With Congenital Torticollis," 120 *Pediatrics* 267 (1992).

16. M. J. Coppes, R. A. Anderson, R. M. Egeler, and J. E. Wolff, "Alternative Therapies for the Treatment of Childhood Cancer," 339 (12) *New Engl. J. Med.* 846 (1998).

17. See, e.g., *Santosky v. Kramer*, 455 U.S. 745 (1982).

Chapter 7

Insurance Reimbursement

Status of Insurance Reimbursement for CAM Therapies

How broadly are CAM therapies such as massage therapy and acupuncture reimbursed by health insurance?

In general, insurance reimbursement for CAM therapies remains largely problematic. Most insurance plans that do claim to "cover" CAM therapies offer discount programs, not benefits. In other words, insureds can receive discounts to CAM practitioners within a network put together by the insurance company, but do not receive insurance reimbursement for CAM services in the same way they might, for example, for a visit to a specialist. Moreover, insurance policies may limit benefits, if any, to specified practitioners (such as acupuncturists only) or to a specified number of visits (such as six chiropractic visits per year). The best thing to do is to read the policy's limitations and exclusions carefully, and/or check with the insurer.

Even if CAM services are covered, though, there are two standard clauses in the typical insurance policy that may preclude reimbursement. The first is a limitation of coverage to treatments that are deemed "medically necessary;" the phrase, while intended to provide a rational limit on insurers' reimbursement obligations, can work to the disadvantage of those insured, since many CAM therapies are, by definition, not "medical."[1] It is often the insurance company, using its own experts on staff, that determines what is "medically necessary" and hence reimbursable. Furthermore, although such a determination ideally would make sense before the patient receives treatment, whether a treatment is "medically necessary" often is decided by the insurance company only after the physician suggests (and sometimes after the patient accepts) a treatment plan, since many insurance contracts reserve to the insurer the right to determine medical necessity after reviewing the case.[2]

The second clause to note is the exclusion for "experimental treatment." Some insurers—and courts in lawsuits regarding insurance decisions—have found CAM therapies such as acupuncture to fall within the "experimental treatment" exception.[3] Finally, because coding systems have not yet been fully adapted (and adopted) to account for CAM therapies, many insurers are unable to offer reimbursement.[4]

Seeking Reimbursement

How can I get insurance reimbursement for CAM therapies such as massage therapy and acupuncture?

In contrast to the above trends, a number of states have enacted legislation that mandates insurance reimbursement for certain CAM therapies and practitioners. At least 46 states, for example, mandate coverage for chiropractic care, and at least six mandate coverage for acupuncture; while many other states have laws that require insurers to reimburse patients for any treatment offered by a licensed CAM practitioner, that would have been reimbursed had the same treatment been offered by a physician or allied health professional.[5] These are frequently known as "any willing provider" or "insurance equity" laws.

Lobbyists are aggressively pursuing efforts to get these kinds of laws enacted in various states.[6] Patients can contact such organizations to find out the status of these grass roots efforts.

In addition, patients can contact professional organizations to become familiar with the laws in their state pertaining to insurance reimbursement for the specific profession (e.g., acupuncture; chiropractic; massage therapy). Patients can also contact their state insurance commissioner regarding the status of current regulations, if any, pertaining to reimbursement for use of CAM therapies.

On the positive side, insurers are increasingly offering some coverage for therapies such as nutritional counseling, biofeedback, acupuncture, chiropractic, and physical therapy.[7] Factors determining whether insurers have decided to cover the therapy include potential cost–effectiveness based on consumer interest, demonstrable clinical efficacy, and state mandates.[8] Thus, a combination of marketplace forces and medical evaluation may be forcing a change in the way insurance organizations handle claims for reimbursement concerning CAM therapies.

References for Chapter 7

1. Cohen (1998), at 103.

2. The argument is made in support of a bill that would expand the definition of medical necessity so as to include CAM therapies. See Medical Necessity Legislation, http://www.healthlobby.com/faim.htm.

3. Cohen (1998), at 102.

4. See generally Alan Dumoff, "A New Code for CAM: HHS Review Could Make Them A Reality," 8(4) Alt. Therapies in Health & Med. 32 (2002).

5. Cohen (1998), at 98.

6. See, for example, the Legislative Update for the Foundation for the Advancement of Innovative Medicine (FAIM), http://www.faim.org).

7. Kennth R. Pelletier, A.R. Marie, M. Krasner, and William L. Haskell, "Current Trends in the Integration and Reimbursement of Complementary and Alternative Medicine by Managed Care, Insurance Carriers, and Hospital Providers," 12(2) Am. J. Health Promot. 112 (1997).

8. Id.; see also Faass (2001), 115–170.

Conclusion

The integration of CAM therapies into conventional medical settings clearly is a growing phenomenon in the U.S., with parallel developments internationally. Increasingly, health care practitioners, institutions, and patients are being required to understand the phenomenon of integrative care, as well as any legal rights and potential liabilities associated with such care.

This book provides an overview of current activity in important arenas of law governing such rights and liabilities. It is based on current developments not only in the law, but also in the medical and other health care professions, as well in professional organizations, lobbying groups, regulatory agencies, and other governmental and non-governmental bodies.

Such developments are continually in flux, and both professional medical advice and legal advice depend on the given circumstances of a specific situation. In the meanwhile, an understanding of the overall picture should help clinicians, institutions, and patients plan the care they offer (or seek) more effectively.

Appendix A

Sample Documentation of Informed Consent

As noted, the form below is merely a model, which must be adapted by an attorney licensed to practice law within the client's state. It includes elements of both informed consent and assumption of risk.

<u>Documentation of Informed Consent</u>

By signing this form, I, [name of patient] agree that [name of clinician] has disclosed to me sufficient information, including the risks and benefits, to enable me to decide to undergo or forgo [name of therapy or course of treatment] for [name of patient's condition].

Our discussion has included: (1) the nature of my condition and procedures to be performed; (2) the nature and probability of material risks involved; (3) benefits to be reasonably expected of the procedure; (4) inability of the practitioner to predict results; (5) irreversibility of the procedure, if that is the case; (6) the likely result of no treatment or procedure; and (7) available alternatives, including their risks and benefits. [Name of clinician] has informed me that he or she has recorded an accurate, written description of the above in my medical record.

I have [refused the following recommended diagnostic and therapeutic interventions, and] elected to use the following [CAM] therapies [list therapies]. [I understand that treatment X is not approved by the federal Food and Drug Administration.]

My consent to this course of treatment is given voluntarily, without coercion, and may be withdrawn, and I am competent and able to understand the nature and consequences of the proposed treatment or procedure.

Assumption of Risk and Release of Liability

The specific risks in making this choice of treatment are: [list of risks provided by clinician]. I knowingly, voluntarily, and intelligently assume these risks and agree to release, indemnify, and defend [name of clinician] and his or her agents from and against any and all claims which I (or my representatives) may have for any loss, damage, or injury arising out of or in connection with my treatment.*

I have carefully read this form and acknowledge that I understand it. No representations, statements, or inducements, oral or written, apart from the foregoing written statement, have been made. This form shall be governed by the laws of the state of [name of state] which shall be the forum for any lawsuits filed under or incident to this form. If any portion of this form is held invalid, the rest of the document shall continue in full force and effect.

_____ [patient signature]   _____ [date]

_____ [clinician signature] _____ [date]

----

* As noted, in some states physicians are not allowed to include an assumption of risk clause, and inclusion of such a clause could, potentially, invalidate the entire agreement.

Appendix B

Sample Documentation for Medical Record

The suggested model below is adapted from the Federation of State Medical Boards Model Guidelines. Its comprehensiveness may or may not appeal to given states or institutions. In any event, such a form, once agreed on, should be completed and signed by the physician or other conventional clinician, and/or included in the medical record, as applicable.

The model form also could be adapted by professional organizations to serve as documentation by non–physician practitioners of CAM therapies, and modified as appropriate and disseminated by health care institutions to help guide various clinicians in an integrative care team.

Accurate and complete clinical records should include the following documentation whenever the clinician counsels the patient regarding CAM therapies or recommends or refers for such therapies:

- the medical history and physical examination;

- diagnostic (conventional and, if applicable, CAM), therapeutic, and laboratory results;

- results of evaluations, consultations, and referrals;

- treatment objectives;

- discussion of risks and benefits;

- appropriate informed consent;

- treatments;

- medications (including date, type, dosage and quantity prescribed);

- instructions and agreements;

- periodic reviews;

- rationale for using CAM therapies, including a notation:

  * as to what medical options have been discussed, offered or tried, and if so, to what effect, or a statement as to whether or not certain options have been refused by the patient or guardian;

  * that proper referral has been offered for appropriate treatment;

  * that the risks and benefits of the use of the recommended treatment to the extent known have been appropriately discussed with the patient or guardian; and,

  * that the physician has determined the extent to which the treatment could interfere with any other recommended or ongoing treatment.

Appendix C

State Licensure of CAM Practitioners

The map of licensure for CAM practitioners changes rapidly, with CAM professional organizations targeting new states and introducing new ideas about licensure—for example, having tiers of practitioners with varying combinations of licensure, certification, and/or registration. Moreover, as noted, new legislation in California, Minnesota, and Rhode Island allows unlicensed CAM practitioners to deliver a variety of health care services. Such legislation is changing the meaning of licensure and eroding the medical profession's historic dominance of health care regulatory as well as delivery systems.

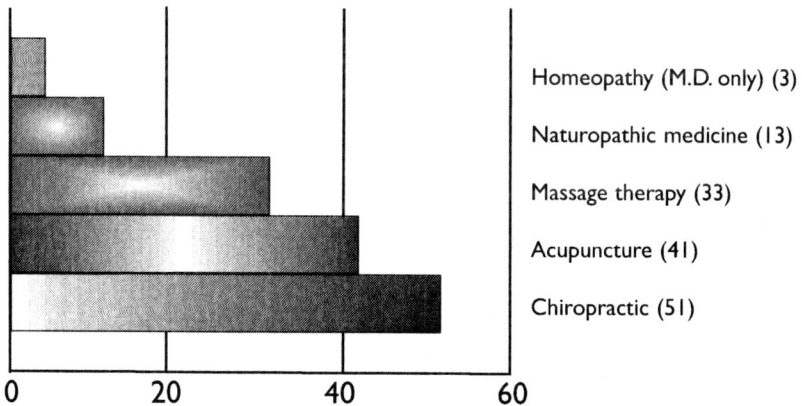

Homeopathy (M.D. only) (3)

Naturopathic medicine (13)

Massage therapy (33)

Acupuncture (41)

Chiropractic (51)

0   20   40   60

The above chart of licensure by state (including the District of Columbia) is based on figures from a variety of sources.[1] The counts differ by source, depending on whether they include regulation other than through state licensing laws (for example, regulation of acupuncture by the state medical board).

References for Appendix C

1. Resources include: *Acupuncture and Oriental Medicine State Laws and Regulations*, available from the National Acupuncture Foundation, http://www.nationalacupuncturefoundation.org; http://www.acupuncture.com; "WSJ Reports Increase in Licensed Naturopaths," (September 2002), http://www.chiroeco.com/news/wsj-more-naturopaths.html).

Appendix D

Sample Syllabus for Continuing Education Talk

Malpractice Liability and Risk Assessment in Complementary and Integrative Medical Therapies

I. Learning Objectives

1. Provide health care professionals and institutions with an overview of potential liability involved in the integration of complementary and alternative medical therapies in clinical practice.

2. Describe the most likely sources of potential exposure and offer some potential tools to help reduce potential liability risk.

3. In so doing, begin to develop a framework for the evolution of legal and regulatory authority governing complementary and integrative medical therapies.

II. Thought Questions for the Audience

Health care law and policy affecting CAM therapies and practitioners are in flux. Although clinicians are beginning to incorporate many CAM therapies, without clear legal, regulatory, and policy guidance, practitioners and institutions, as well as patients, operate in an uncertain and hazardous legal environment. Presently, at least seven interrelated areas of law affect legal and policy decisions surrounding clinical integration of CAM into conventional care. These include: (1) credentialing and licensure; (2) scope of practice; (3) malpractice liability; (4) food and drug law; (5) professional discipline; (6) insurance reimbursement rules; and (7) rules governing health care fraud.

The talk focuses on legal rules relevant to potential malpractice liability for complementary/integrative care, proposes a framework within which clinicians can assess liability risk, and offers specific liability management strategies. The talk addresses counseling patients regarding CAM therapies, and the referral of patients to CAM practitioners. The questions such individuals and organizations must address include:

1. Who will likely get sued?

2. What kinds of protective measures will allow responsible, clinical integration of CAM therapies while minimizing risks of civil liability, criminal prosecution, or professional discipline?

3. What is the liability for referral of the patient to a CAM practitioner?

4. To what extent are liabilities by various practitioners shared in integrative medicine centers?

5. How important is it for various individuals and institutions to understand credentialing systems applicable to CAM practitioners? To what extent may non-licensed practitioners (such as herbalists and homeopaths in some cases) be included in insurance and referral networks?

6. What are the relevant elements of an appropriate, informed consent disclosure, and when is lack of disclosure likely to trigger potential liability?

7. What are the most important risk management strategies for the clinician? How can these be implemented within the institution?

Several suggestions will be made to help create a more legally defensible practice environment. For example, attention to documentation including appropriate informed consent can help reduce risk. Similarly, thought should be given to keeping backup files of medical literature justifying therapeutic choices involving CAM modalities. It should be noted that the talk is educational in nature and does not purport to give legal advice or opinion.

Rather, these are general strategies for implementation. Legal counsel should be consulted for advice or an opinion in any given context.

There is a crucial need to provide leadership in legal and regulatory developments to serve hospitals, academic medical centers, educational institutions, and federal, state, and local governments who are creating law and setting policy.

The legal issues raised by CAM therapies overlap with clinical considerations and, although amenable to resolution on a practitioner-by-practitioner or institutional basis, ideally require resolution at a national, if not international level. Many nations outside the U.S., for example, are committed to helping to maintain and promote traditional healing systems and to facilitating a sensible integration of such systems with biomedical care. The question is whether legal and regulatory structures are evolving to support shifts in health care by recognizing the many legitimate facets of the person's search for wholeness.

III. Resources
(See also endnote references throughout book.)

Papers & Articles

White House Commission on Complementary and Alternative Medicine Policy. *Executive Summary, Final Report* (2002).

Federal Trade Commission. *Dietary Supplements: An Advertising Guide for Industry.* http://www.ftc.gov

Food and Drug Administration. *Regulations on Statements Made for Dietary Supplements Concerning the Effect of the Product on the Structure or Function of the Body.* 21 CFR Part 101, 65:4 Fed Reg 1000 (Jan. 6, 2000).

Marcus, D. M. & Grollman, A. P., Botanical Medicines: The Need for New Regulations. 347:25 *New Engl. J. Med.* 2073 (2002).

McNamara, S.H., Regulation of dietary supplements. *New Engl. J. Med.* 343 (17):1270, 2000 Oct 26.

Books

Callahan, D., ed., *The Role of Complementary & Alternative Medicine: Accommodating Pluralism*. Washington, D.C.: Georgetown University Press, 2002.

Cohen, Michael H., *Complementary and Alternative Medicine: Legal Boundaries and Regulatory Perspectives*. Baltimore, M.D.: Johns Hopkins University Press, 1998.

Cohen, Michael H., *Beyond Complementary Medicine: Legal and Ethical Perspectives on Health Care and Human Evolution*. Ann Arbor, MI: University of Michigan Press, 2000.

Cohen, Michael H., *Future Medicine*. Ann Arbor, MI: University of Michigan Press, 2003.

Ernst, E.E., Pittler, M.H., Stevinson, C., & White, A. *The Desktop Guide to Complementary and Alternative Medicine: an Evidence-Based Approach*. London: Harcourt Publishers Ltd., 2001; 444 pages.

Slater, V. & Rankin-Box, D. *The Nurses' Handbook of Complementary Therapies*. New York: Churchill–Livingstone, 1996.

Selected Government Web Sites

FDA: http://vm.cfsan.fda.gov/~dms/supplmnt.html

FTC: http://www.ftc.gov/bcp/conline/pubs/buspubs/dietsupp.htm

NIH: http://ods.od.nih.gov/databases/ibids.html

NLM: http://www.nlm.nih.gov/services/dietsup.html

USDA: http://www.nalusda.gov/fnic/etext/000015.html

USP: http://www.usp.org

White House Commission on Complementary and Alternative Medicine Policy:
        http://www.whccamp.hhs.gov

Index

Index

About the Author

Michael H. Cohen is Director of Legal Programs at the Harvard Medical School Osher Institute and the Division for Research and Education in Complementary and Integrative Medical Therapies. He serves as Lecturer on Medicine in the Department of Medicine, Harvard Medical School and a Fortieth Anniversary Scholar at the Center for the Study of World Religions, Harvard Divinity School. He has taught "Health Law & Policy: Complementary and Alternative Medicine" at the Harvard School of Public Health.

He received his J.D. from Boalt Hall School of Law, University of California, Berkeley, his M.B.A. from the Haas School of Management, University of California, Berkeley, his M.F.A. from the Iowa Writers' Workshop, University of Iowa, and his B.A. from Columbia University. He served as a law clerk to Judge Thomas P. Griesa in the United States District Court for the Southern District of New York, practiced corporate law at Davis Polk & Wardwell, a Wall Street law firm, and as law professor, taught health care law. He is a member of the Bar in the states of California, New York, Massachusetts, and Washington, D.C.

He is the author of numerous scholarly articles and of several books, including: *Complementary and Alternative Medicine: Legal Boundaries and Regulatory Perspectives* (Johns Hopkins University Press, 1998); *Beyond Complementary Medicine: Legal and Ethical Perspectives on Health Care and Human Evolution* (University of Michigan Press, 2000); and *Future Medicine: Ethical Challenges, Regulatory Dilemmas, and Therapeutic Pathways to Health and Healing in Human Transformation* (University of Michigan Press, 2003).

Resources and current contact information are available through his Web site, www.camlawblog.com.